BECAUSE YOU ARE SUPERWOMAN

HOW TO HARNESS YOUR SUPERPOWER AND CREATE YOUR OWN POSITIVE BIRTH EXPERIENCE WITH MINIMAL MEDICAL INTERVENTION

J.K. COY

Copyright © 2018 J.K. Coy
All rights reserved.
ISBN-13: 978-1727141009
ISBN-10: 1727141008

The method (The Six Steps to a Minimal Intervention (M.I.) Birth™) and the terminology (M.I. Birth™), were created by J.K. Coy.

All rights reserved. No part of this book may be reproduced or transmitted in any form or by any means, electronic or mechanical, including photocopying, recording or by an information storage and retrieval system — except for brief quotations in a review to be printed in a magazine, newspaper or on the Web.

You must not rely on the information in this book as an alternative to medical advice from your doctor or other professional healthcare provider.

If you have any specific questions about any medical matter you should consult your doctor or other professional healthcare provider.

If you think you may be suffering from any medical condition you should seek immediate medical attention.

You should never delay seeking medical advice, disregard medical advice, or discontinue medical treatment because of information in this book.

Editing by Elizabeth Hess

Cover Design by Mykola Shelepa

Please visit MyMomistheWorst.com
for more stories and products related to or mentioned in this book.

DEDICATION

"A great teacher helps her students find their strengths and learn to believe in themselves; because at the end of the day, she knows they ultimately have to do the hardest work on their own."
— J.K. Coy

While the major task of physically birthing my two little loves was mine, it was the calm and confidence that my husband and midwife instilled in me that helped me cross the finish line on a "birth high," despite my initial fears about giving birth and my body's ability to do it without intervention. Thank you for teaching me to believe in myself.

CONTENTS

ACKNOWLEDGMENTS	5
1 CLAIMING YOUR SUPERPOWER	6
2 HOW YOU FEEL ABOUT BIRTH MATTERS	17
3 YOUR BIRTH CHOICES MATTER:	32
INCLUDING **THE SIX STEPS TO YOUR OWN MINIMAL INTERVENTION (M.I.) BIRTH**	42
4 YOUR BIRTH STORY MATTERS	66
5 JADE'S BIRTH STORY: TAKING CONTROL OF MY HEALTH TO FIND MY INNER SUPERHERO	74
6 SARAH'S BIRTH STORIES: YOUR CARE CAN BE PERSONAL	100
7 HOLLIE'S BIRTH STORIES: I KEPT TRYING FOR THE BIRTH EXPERIENCE I WANTED	116
8 MARTHA'S BIRTH STORIES: YOUR BIRTH TEAM PLAYS A VITAL ROLE IN HOW YOU FEEL ABOUT YOUR EXPERIENCE	128
9 STEPHANIE'S BIRTH STORY: "TYPE A" HAS THREE EPIDURAL-FREE INDUCTIONS	136
10 MEGHAN'S BIRTH STORY: FIND YOUR SUPPORT TEAM SO YOU CAN DO GREAT THINGS	147
11 PAT'S BIRTH STORIES: FROM MI TO CA; THREE FANTASTIC BIRTHS WITH MY DOCTOR'S FULL SUPPORT	159

12 JOANN'S BIRTH STORY: WHAT BIRTH LOOKS LIKE IN A COUNTRY WHERE NATURAL IS THE NORM	168
13 HEATHER'S BIRTH STORY: FROM THE BOARD ROOM TO THE DELIVERY ROOM	183
14 TINA'S BIRTH STORY: BEING YOUR OWN BIRTH ADVOCATE IS CHALLENGING, BUT HIGHLY WORTH IT!	188
15 ANNA'S BIRTH STORY: HAVING AN "ADVANCED MATERNAL AGE" DOESN'T MAKE YOUR BODY INCAPABLE	204
16 TAHLIA'S BIRTH STORIES: GIVE ME MORE (BABIES, NOT DRUGS)!	211
17 JACQUELYN'S BIRTH STORY: WHO SAYS A TWIN BIRTH MUST USE MAXIMUM INTERVENTIONS?	226
18 JACLYN'S BIRTH STORIES: FROM FEARING BIRTH TO INSPIRING STORIES OF INTERVENTION-FREE BIRTHS	237
19 GET EXCITED, BECAUSE YOU WERE MADE FOR THIS!	258
I WANT TO HEAR FROM YOU	261
READ MORE TITLES BY J.K. COY	262
ABOUT THE AUTHOR	263
RESOURCES	264

ACKNOWLEDGMENTS

Every day, this book teaches and inspires women how to achieve a positive birth experience with little or no medical interventions.

It sounds like a nice pipe dream until you read about the women **just like you** that are achieving positive, minimal intervention births. I am incredibly thankful to the passionate and bold women in this book who shared their birth experiences (in epic detail) so that we can change the way women and medical professionals think about, talk about, and practice birth in this country.

1 CLAIMING YOUR SUPERPOWER

My husband likes to refer to me as "Superwoman."

Of course, no spouse constantly feels this way about their other half. I am highly aware that I have plenty of shortcomings. But when the subject of birth comes up, he likes to remind me how amazing it was to witness his wife being so incredibly strong and capable as we welcomed our daughters into the world.

It was two intervention-free hospital births in the last two years that earned me that designation. But painting myself as a strong, brave heroine isn't the full picture. I am also the preschool wimp who got one ear pierced and then jumped into the store's window display to hide because I was so filled with fear just anticipating the pain of the second poke. I actually refused to get the other ear pierced until the fourth grade.

BECAUSE YOU ARE SUPERWOMAN

Don't worry, my mom did take out the lone earring to spare me from looking like a tiny pirate. No one wants their little girl to have to explain that she is a big wimp every time someone notices her pirate ear. Thanks, Mom.

So obviously, anticipating the pain of childbirth for over thirty years had me terrified. I assumed that when the day came my water would break somewhere wildly embarrassing. Then, with water dripping between my legs, I'd rush right to the hospital in a panic, screaming for the epidural the moment they sat me in a wheel chair. Then I'd lay on my back with my legs spread eagle, cursing my husband's name for DOING THIS TO ME! The doctor would rush in just in time to catch my camera-ready newborn baby, and the nightmare would be over!

Honestly, that was one of the only common birth examples I had ever been exposed to. On the very rare occasion that someone brought up a story involving a woman going au natural or desiring minimal medical interventions, it was surrounded by snide comments, alluding to the notion that the woman and her birth were a bit…crazy, granola, hippy, old-fashioned, uneducated, unplanned or reckless in the face of modern medicine.

My own sister-in-law had two home births after a tough hospital birth, so you would think I would have some other reference point. But she also now lives on a mountain in rural Argentina, so she is obviously a unique breed. It was difficult for me to relate to her and her "natural ways" when I finally

7

found myself in need of childbirth advice. In fact, since we were really nothing alike, I assumed birthing without intervention wasn't for me.

Me (Probably a Lot Like You)

I've spent years learning from higher instruction, earning degrees in business and education. I've worked in professional environments for a decade and a half. I have a fairly progressive husband who willingly jumps in to help maintain the details of managing our household. Our finances are in order (*meaning,* I at least track my spending enough to know that I have burned through way too much of my daughter's college education money at coffee shops as I pen this book). I've created a modest, yet comfortable, Pinterest-worthy home for my sensible family of four and our rescue companion, an elderly red dog that looks more like a dingo.

Alright, enough with the gold stars. We're all bored.

But all that said, it is not unfathomable that I resist my intervention-free births being categorized as crazy, granola, hippy, old-fashioned, uneducated, unplanned, or reckless.

And I'm not the only one.

The New Examples of Birth

In this book you'll read over twenty stories of amazing

who had positive birth experiences, all requiring very
intervention from modern medicine. These women
have conquered their own self-doubt. They have stared down
the deepest parts of childbirth, and now, you get to be a fly on
the wall as you transport yourself into their stories and see
how they found their own strength to kick childbirth squarely
between the eyes.

The women in this book, myself included, are strong,
educated, modern mamas who wanted more options to
achieve a positive and healthy birth experience for them and
their babies. Just like you, we had questions. We wanted to
understand the "why" of our care. We wanted the evidence,
and then we wanted to feel supported to make decisions with
our family's interests in mind. We did not want to make our
birth decisions out of fear. When we looked at how modern
medicine had overstepped its boundaries, we insisted on
something better.

Just because birth interventions are so common that they are
now considered normal, we knew that didn't actually mean
they were necessary or beneficial for us. They were not
accepted as our standard for care.

Alternatively, we all knew how fortunate we were to have
modern medicine as our back-up in case we were truly part of
the small minority that should require intervention.

Some Alarming Intervention Data

According to the National Listening to Mothers Survey (2013), which interviewed over two thousand women who had birthed in the prior year, interventions in labor were closely linked to increased, unplanned cesareans. Specifically, the study noted women who received an induction or epidural were more likely to have an unplanned c-section. The most common forms of induction they referenced were the use of synthetic oxytocin (Pitocin), breaking a woman's waters, inserting a finger into the cervix and "sweeping" or "stripping" the membranes, or a prostaglandin gel, pouch, or tablet placed near the cervix. Often times, women receive an induction concoction that includes two or more of these methods.

The idea that one intervention increases the likelihood of others, is often referred to as the "cascade of intervention." Once interventions are introduced, the unplanned cesarean rate increases. Among first-time mothers who had term births and experienced labor, those who had both labor induction and an epidural were *six times* more likely to have a c-section (31%) than those who had neither intervention (5%). Get out your highlighter and make sure that last sentence is glowing.

Additionally, there are plenty of other routine birth practices that have become par for the course but show little benefit to a laboring woman: restricting food intake, using bladder catheters, restricted movement while attached to intravenous fluids, time constraints, continuous electronic fetal monitoring, and lying flat on our backs to push.

Reserving Interventions for Plan B

Please understand, I am not here to tell you that medical interventions are the devil. I am not on some witch hunt, crusading for women to deny all assistance during birth. I would like to assume these interventions were created with good intentions in mind. The problem lies in the fact that most interventions have become synonymous with childbirth in this country. And many have become widely used out of convenience, instead of necessity. Interventions have become the Plan A; the starting point for birth. As women, we have stopped asking "Why?" and started accepting that this is just what birth looks like in this country.

Unfortunately, this passive acceptance has come at a cost.

Medical practitioners perform cesareans at approximately 32% of U.S. births. That is almost one in three births that end with major surgery. Ultimately, cesareans have become the most commonly performed surgery in this country. It feels like that should be a red flag, birth in this country is in a bit of a crisis.

In fact, our cesarean rate is more than double what the World

Health Organization recommends to reach the most favorable outcomes in decreasing the maternal and infant mortality rate. Staci Berrey, a doula for almost a decade, and owner of Labor of Love Birth Services in Orange County, CA, explained, "Medical intervention is not the enemy; it is the overuse of it for reasons that show little benefit to the laboring mother that we should take issue with."

Interventions save mothers and their babies every day, but we should question whose best interest is being put first when an intervention is the starting point for birth in modern medicine. If we prepare a woman's mind and body, make her feel safe and supported, and then get out of her way, the body is amazing and actually knows how to birth with very little assistance or intervention. If we were able to save costs on unnecessary interventions upfront, that would leave more money available for a woman's follow-up care after delivery. One way to do this could be reducing the cesarean rate, since c-sections are fifty percent more costly to providers than vaginal births.

It should be noted that the United States has the highest maternal death rate among developed nations. Over sixty percent of maternal deaths are preventable with regular monitoring of the mother. After giving birth twice, I fully believe that waiting four to six weeks for a woman's first postpartum check-up is far too long, especially since in the same time frame it is common to have three or more appointments centered around your newborn.

A Mental Shift

When I found out I was pregnant with my first, I spent the first thirty-two weeks under the care of a traditional OB-GYN, who I actually really liked. But once I started to learn that my birth choices were greater than…

- A tree-hugging, drug-free, painful birth or medical interventions as soon as I reached the hospital?
- A home birth with no aide or a hospital birth where someone else made choices for me based on dated practices?
- How soon did I want to be induced or would I rather just schedule a c-section?
- An epidural or pure hell?

I started picturing the possibility of a minimal intervention, positive birth experience, based on the principles and practices of believing in what my body was made to do (while not being embarrassed to admit I was totally open to evidence-based medical interventions that became necessary).

With this mental shift, I knew I needed to switch to be under the care of a woman who was experienced in advocating for using only those interventions that were in a woman's, and her baby's, best interest. Someone who routinely saw the miracle that our bodies are capable of with very little aide. Someone who truly believed that most medical interventions did not need to be common practice and would best be saved for Plan B, after first supporting me with less invasive techniques.

I knew that for me to fully trust someone during a time when I could feel scared and vulnerable, it would be critical to have someone in charge of the show who knew what was "normal" during a birth where medical intervention was an option, but a road taken only after a number of other more natural methods were exhausted.

The Birth Dialogue

If we want to change birth in this country, we need to change the dialogue surrounding it. Birth doesn't have to be traumatizing. Each woman sharing her story in this book truly believes that. We want to empower you with confidence in your mind and body. We want to give you the courage to seek a positive birth experience beyond the horror stories that society has routinely exposed us to. This means educating yourself with new perspectives of birth and seeking out care providers who specifically align with your goals. Our childbirth beliefs have such a profound impact on the care choices we make, on the way we labor, on our outcomes, and ultimately how we feel about our experience.

My Great Aunt Pat shared her positive, intervention-free, hospital birth story with me long before I was pregnant. She didn't tell me it was orgasmic. She didn't say it was easy. She didn't say it was painless. But she did say it was totally, one hundred percent worth it. In fact, she chose to birth the same way two more times. At the end of her story, she turned to me with delight in her voice and said, "You could totally do it, too!"

Her words spoke power into me. She believed in me before I had even considered believing in myself. Because the confidence was coming from a strong woman who had fully experienced birth and spoke positively about it, I trusted it.

But I was still nervous. How could she believe I could do something so unfathomable? Births like that are for superheroes. They are rare unicorns. They are for totally-committed natural mamas. They are for people so much stronger than me. But words are powerful, and the notion stuck with me.

A few years later, I found myself pregnant, and I recalled her confidence in me. I wasn't sure what it all meant, but little by little, I started to put aside what I thought I knew about birth. By reading the mind-blowing stories of women who didn't curse birth, but instead believed in their bodies and took charge of their care, I started letting go of the notion that childbirth was just some tragic event that women had to endure. Instead, I started getting excited about the life transforming power women can experience through childbirth.

By harnessing the confidence and techniques I learned from other remarkable women who had succeeded in the type of birth experience I wanted, I was able to create my own positive examples of birth as I welcomed my daughters into the world. The same six techniques I used (laid out in detail in chapter three) can be replicated by anyone who wants their own minimal intervention birth. The journey began when someone opened my mind to the possibility of a positive birth experience and then instilled confidence in me with their positive words. From there, the responsibility fell on me to be an active participant in my care choices.

I want to pay it forward. I want to provide that same confidence to you. I believe in you. I believe in your body. I believe it is okay for you to stand up and ask questions. I believe you deserve a positive birth experience. You are an incredible, educated, strong, modern woman with a body that is capable of giving birth. Each of the women in this book believe in you. You are not too weak, too old, too broken, or too scared to just roll over and let birth happen to you. You have superwoman inside you.

It's time you believe it.

2 HOW YOU FEEL ABOUT BIRTH MATTERS

The very minute you are reading this, eight babies are being born in the U.S. That's almost 11,000 babies per day. Those are a lot of warm, snuggly newborns (and diapers)!

Now, pause for a moment.

All those babies, yet when is the last time you heard anyone talking about the act of giving birth in a positive context?

There is an accepted dialogue around birth in this country. Birth is scary, painful, unnatural, should unfold in a perfect pattern, and it demands medical intervention. It feels like birth has been reduced to a negative experience that women are better off avoiding by means of every medical intervention offered.

We have to be careful. Words are incredibly powerful. They

have the power to shape the way we feel and what we believe about birth, which in turn shapes the choices we make, and ultimately shapes our labor and delivery experiences. The way we talk about birth and the type of birth stories we share actually have the opportunity to change outcomes.

The outcome of how women feel about their bodies. The outcome of the care that women begin to demand. The outcome of what is considered standard medical procedure in birth. The outcome of our country's elevated cesarean rate.

Giving Out Negative Birth Stories like Wedding Gifts

Just mention childbirth in a room full of women, then count to three. Women practically fall over each other, like single ladies leaping toward a hurled wedding bouquet, to share their birth stories. But whether we realize it or not, women are more comfortable sharing their horror stories than their hero stories. The positive stories get minimized and the negative stories get amplified, even though it is obvious, that if asked, we would unanimously agree that we want to be part of the club that had a positive birth experience.

Similarly, an ugly divorce always seems to get more word of mouth action than a happy marriage of thirty years. But if asked, we would surely say we would desire the latter for ourselves. If we really want something better, wouldn't it make sense to steal wisdom from a happily married couple while we still have the opportunity?

Childbirth is no different. We need to share positive birth stories so that people know they exist and so they can understand how they can achieve one.

Whether your birth story is au natural or ends in a marvel of modern medicine, if you feel educated and supported before, during, and after your birth, you will likely have a positive birth story to share. But reaching your own positive birth experience will require some investment of your time and energy. Like the example of a positive marriage, if you ask anyone who has one, it doesn't "just happen."

Honestly, What Do You Think About Birth?

Yesterday, I was sipping wine among a few friends I keep around who do not have children. I like to live vicariously through their spontaneous weekend getaways, and the variety of our conversations remind me that I used to talk about things other than boobs, poop, and cartoons. Sometimes, they get to snuggle a cute, squishy baby to get their fix and then pass her back when she smells foul. It works out for everyone. We all know what we bring to the table. So, I raised the notion of childbirth to gauge the dialogues they have heard and how they felt about the idea of giving birth someday.

The views they expressed can best be described as "scared sh*tless" about the idea of giving birth. They talked about the pain, fear, and horror stories that other women had poured into them.

That's a grim starting point for any woman, especially the 11,000 that will give birth today! However, I can totally relate to the feelings and stories my friends were sharing. I would have been right there, agreeing along with them, just a few years ago. I had no other version in my head about what childbirth was like. Woman to woman, I was always being told how awful birth was until it was over, or at least until the godsend of the epidural was inserted! I just thought every woman must be scarred by her birth. I had been taught to believe negative birth experiences were as guaranteed as growing older.

But truly, how could we even have a mental basis for another possible outcome? The way women talk about birth, we are conditioned to believe there is no way we can, or should want to, fully experience it. We should accept every intervention as early as possible, to avoid dealing with any and all aspects of the dreaded act of childbirth.

Turns out, that is poor advice.

Birth can actually be a beautiful, positive experience that empowers the laboring woman by teaching her the strength her mind and body possess! It can also be a calm, healthy, first bonding experience that a mother and child get to enjoy together. But for those kinds of experiences to be a reality for more women, we will need to start doing birth differently than we currently do it.

If our society did a better job of instilling trust in women and

BECAUSE YOU ARE SUPERWOMAN

their bodies, the rest of us could stop making our birth decisions out of fear!

Replacing the Current Birth Dialogue with Something Better

Several relational studies have concluded that for every negative interaction, we must experience multiple positive interactions to cancel out the effects from the negative interaction. One of the most famous studies on this topic was produced by John Gottman, a psychological researcher who did extensive work over four decades on divorce prediction and marital stability. He studied hundreds of wedded couples in an effort to understand their likelihood of staying married or ending in divorce. His study uncovered that one of the biggest success indicators to a lasting marriage was the ratio of positive and negative verbal and nonverbal interactions that partners had with each other. He concluded the optimal ratio was five positive interactions to every one negative interaction. Without that ratio, confidence and happiness in the marriage declined.

Positive words and interactions are absurdly powerful. If you want to help a pregnant woman out, please tell her something good! Send her a card that says how much you believe in her, how strong her body is, and how much of a bad*ss she is; build her up! And to all the incredible, pregnant women reading this book, I want to tell you the kindest thing another woman ever said to me when I was pregnant, and it is my wish for you too, "I hope you have a quick and easy delivery!"

And even if labor doesn't quite go down like this in the end, this ideal is much more fun to fantasize about for nine months than the alternative!

Those words are so simple, yet they are exactly what you are hoping for as you reach the end of pregnancy. That message is one example of what you need to hear to help you stay positive and keep a level head. I don't know why we don't say and hear things like that more often surrounding birth, but now you get to spread sweet, simple, and uplifting messages to other mamas and make their day.

Think about it, a sane woman wouldn't recount the details of her ugly divorce to a bride just weeks before her wedding day. I don't know why some women think it is totally appropriate to share their negative birth experiences with every pregnant mama on the verge of delivery.

But realistically, not all women have their own positive birth story to share. If we want to change the way women feel about childbirth, we have to give them positive examples of what birth can be and tools to help them achieve their own.

We have a long way to go to sway the birth discussion and diffuse the unnecessary negativity that surrounds childbirth in this country, but we absolutely can!

Taking Back Your Voice in Birth

We are in this mess because we started avoiding as much about birth as humanly possible, and that was not the right answer. We were aiming to avoid the experience instead of embracing it.

It may seem absurdly rare in light of the negative stories that circulate, but many women do have positive birth experiences; they just haven't been encouraged to share them. Women don't typically feel comfortable sharing their positive birth experiences, or their desire for positive birth experiences, in a room full of naysayers. At times, we have trouble finding our voice. The voice to question accepted birth practices that show little scientific evidence of benefiting the mother or her baby. The voice to stand up and share our positive birth story. The voice to tell other women we believe a positive birth experience is possible. The voice to say we want better and we expect better.

It was less than one hundred years ago that women gained the right and voice to vote throughout this country, though we now tend to take it for granted. It wasn't until 1920 that the nineteenth amendment was solidified, officially stating that our right to vote is not determined by our gender. After hundreds of years of prior oppression, women have inherently had trouble standing up for themselves. But the last century has brought incredible opportunities for women to carve new perspectives and actions. It is time we assertively take childbirth back into our own hands.

Realistic Birth Expectations

Changing the way we talk about birth doesn't mean we have to paint a picture that childbirth is easy or painless. The last thing I want is a woman to make her birth decisions casually and then feel unprepared when the moment of truth sets in.

A woman shared with me that she had decided she wanted a natural birth, but then back labor set in, and she crumbled. She said she came out feeling like a failure. I do not want you to feel like a failure. Instead, I want to prepare you for a positive experience. I want to set you on a path toward the best possible outcome. In the next chapter, I will provide you with the six steps to reach a minimal intervention birth. You will have the specific tools, and then you will have to decide which to set in motion. You have the opportunity to set your mind and body up for success through the stories and beliefs you fill it with and the type of care you demand. Beyond that, you will need to leave room for a little grace. You can't fully control how your baby arrives earth side. Even you Type A mamas who already have your unborn child signed up for preschool. Bless your heart.

Many people decide that because there are elements they can't control, they are better off leaving things completely open, avoiding a plan like the plague. I have to say, I think that is silly.

New and challenging things should require a bit of a leap, a coach, and an action plan. Let's think about this from a fitness goal perspective. If you had never run a mile before, and you told all your friends and coworkers that you signed up for a half marathon, but you weren't going to train or plan for it because you couldn't control your body on the day of the race, they would think you were nuts! In their minds, they would assume you were destined to fail. They'd probably try to encourage you toward a training plan or a coach, if they cared about you and your success. Or more likely, they would just encourage you not to do it at all.

Even if you did end up hiring a coach and following a training plan, you couldn't guarantee yourself success. You still might sprain your ankle at mile nine (unlikely, but possible). At that point, I assume you would be pretty frustrated, but I doubt you would feel like a failure. You would understand that what happened was out of your control. You would understand that statistically you put yourself in the best possible situation to finish well because you had a plan, a coach, and trained accordingly. You achieved nine miles more than you ever did in a race before, and next time, you will be in a much better position to crush the entire race. If you completed all that, I doubt you would tell other people that running was a huge mistake. You would still feel pretty accomplished.

Similarly, if you commit to the six steps for a minimal intervention birth, you will greatly increase your chance at a minimal intervention birth experience. You will have no reason to feel like a failure if intervention ends up being a necessary outcome because you will know that you first tried implementing the best evidence-based practices to reduce intervention. You will be thankful that modern medicine was available when it was needed.

Preparing for Plan A and remaining open to Plan B puts you in the perfect spot to achieve a positive birth experience. You can't be so casual that you say you want something but then put little to no effort in, scared away at the first sign of something you didn't plan on. And you can't be so rigid that you forget to use the brain you were given if major roadblocks appear. Having a completely inflexible mindset puts an incredible amount of stress on you, and fear and stress do not encourage babies to come out. The day you meet your child is supposed to be a joyous occasion, not something that you are so afraid of you find yourself crying into your pillow each night that you get closer to birth day.

Thinking back to each of my pregnancies, I really did want a positive, intervention-free, natural (as it is commonly referred to) birth experience, but I was a little scared to shout it from the rooftops because I didn't know how to go after it or how realistic it was. I needed specific action steps to feel more comfortable with the idea.

After two intervention-free births in less than two years and countless hours of evidence-based research, I decided to record what worked. The six steps have become known as the **Minimal Intervention (M.I.) Birth Method**.

In this book, I will share with you the six specific action steps you can use to take control of your own **Minimal Intervention (M.I.) Birth**. This method prepares you to go after your positive birth experience while remaining open to the idea of using medical interventions that become a necessity.

In short, prepare to do your best, then ride out the rest.

If that birth motto doesn't already come cross-stitched on a pillow, someone please do me a favor and get on that!

Starting Positive Birth Dialogues

Childbirth is something you only get to experience a few times in your life, but it tends to be a defining experience that you will reference over and over again. I congratulate you for reading this book and committing to invest some time and energy in the planning of your care, your labor, and the delivery of your child.

After two positive birth experiences where I felt safe, strong, and capable, I know that childbirth doesn't have to be negative, feared, or avoided. It can actually be a wonderful experience shared among women.

Once I started to share my birth stories with other women, it opened a door for them to share their own positive birth experiences. I realized it wasn't that no positive birth experiences existed, and it wasn't that pregnant women didn't want to have them. It was that women who had them hadn't been encouraged to share them, and women who wanted them weren't sure who to ask.

One woman confided that she felt bad sharing her positive birth story because when she had shared it in the past, other women discounted her experience, implying she had made it up. Not the birth part, of course, but the part that she believed her childbirth experience was positive and empowering *not* just because of the cute, squishy baby she received at the end.

That is an incredible shame. It was a positive experience that got turned into something she was embarrassed to talk about because some women didn't understand how to be happy for someone else in light of their own crumby experiences. It's negativity like that that holds women's views of birth from advancing. Unfortunately, it does help explain why we tend to only get one side of the birth story—and it's not the positive one.

But how can we expect women to speak positively about birth if they have never had an empowering experience or heard positive examples of what birth can be? For that reason, I chose to interview the amazing women in this book. Their stories have the power to open your mind to what fully experiencing birth can be like, reshaping your birth beliefs along the way.

Your Chance to Give (and Get) Positive Birth Examples

I want to open up the mic to women who have something positive to say about birth. To those who are fed-up with the fear and negativity surrounding childbirth, you have the chance to change the conversation about birth in this county. Together, we can start a collection of positive beliefs about birth for women of all ages to reference.

To get involved, tag **@StoriesbyJKCoy**, or use the hashtags listed via social media in your positive birth posts. I will regularly be featuring these tagged posts, as well as using them to choose some fierce females to receive fun swag, and even possibly a spot in a future birth book!

If you're pregnant, take a bump pic and let us know how far along you are so we can all encourage you as you prepare for your upcoming birth!

This kind of collaboration will take our individual thoughts and experiences, and help them come together to create a positive birth momentum.

Let other women know what you stand for. Share positive, transformational thinking. Think of it as a gift to yourselves, your friends, and your future daughters (or sons).

I have very vivid dreams. So much so that my husband cuts me off when I begin to mention one of the dreams I had the night before because he says I get too "worked up." It's true, I do. But I'm not even mad about it, I like to think of it as passion.

Here are some of the positive birth dialogues I've dreamed up...

- Half-way to meeting this little gift #20wks. Please send all the positive birth vibes my way! #BecauseYouAreSuperwoman #MIBirth @StoriesbyJKCoy
- 32 weeks today. Believing in my body's ability to give birth, since it has already proven its amazing ability to grow this human! #BecauseYouAreSuperwoman #MIBirth @StoriesbyJKCoy
- Teaching women that a positive birth experience is possible should be our country's first form of birth intervention. #BecauseYouAreSuperwoman #MIBirth @StoriesbyJKCoy
- Busy filling my head with positive birth stories thanks to this book! #BecauseYouAreSuperwoman #MIBirth @StoriesbyJKCoy
- A shout out to my amazing support team during labor. Thank you for believing in me and supporting my goals to achieve the best experience possible. #BecauseYouAreSuperwoman #MIBirth @StoriesbyJKCoy
- I did it! I'm sharing my positive birth story so that people know positive birth experiences DO exist... #BecauseYouAreSuperwoman #MIBirth @StoriesbyJKCoy

- Ladies (pregnant or not), you need to check out this book! It will change the way you think about birth. #BecauseYouAreSuperwoman #MIBirth @StoriesbyJKCoy

Feel free to copy these (copying is still one of the sincerest forms of flattery; I'm already getting butterflies!), or come up with something much wittier and more inspiring.

I want to be part of a future where women's birth stories are celebrated, women believe in their bodies, and women demand that evidence-based practices are part of the birth care equation. A country where our cesarean rates and labor costs have dramatically decreased, maternal care is increased, and women's views on labor and delivery grow from positive birth examples.

I can vividly picture myself basking in the warm sun on the patio of a quaint little coffee shop with my two grown daughters, sipping overpriced iced lattes and telling them the stories of how empowering and beautiful their births were for their mother. They will likely sigh, because like a good mother does, I've told them the same story millions of times. But they will also know that they have the same beautiful opportunity in their future, if they so choose.

I sincerely wish the same for you and your family.

3 YOUR BIRTH CHOICES MATTER

INCLUDING THE SIX STEPS TO ACHIEVE A MINIMAL INTERVENTION BIRTH

Hold up. This may be a birth book, but there is something you should probably know about me. I get really squeamish around anything medical.

I don't like visiting the doctor. I don't like feeling like a patient. I can't even enjoy watching fictional emergency room television shows. I can never cover my eyes quick enough when some type of bodily fluid starts spraying everywhere (and it always does)!

Many of my family members actually work in hospitals: grandmas, aunts, cousins, nieces, *my own mother*. I plug my ears when they share medical stories at the dinner table. No one needs a blood and gore story to wash down their chicken salad.

When it comes to medication, I've always erred on the side of less is more. We've all seen that commercial for medication to treat an overactive bladder where the list of possible side effects scrolls on and on: irregular heartbeat, internal bleeding, depression, weight gain, and a droopy left eye. The side effects sound far worse than the ailment that the medicine is supposed to treat. The good news is by the end of the commercial, you are almost content to just keep your overactive bladder.

And then there was middle school. I pretty much blacked out during health class. There was way too much information about the inner workings of my uterus, cervix, and ovaries. I'd probably fail miserably if you asked me to identify each of their locations on a diagram, but apparently, they work. I got pregnant. Twice.

In my early twenties, I moved to a new city and started my first big girl job which offered health insurance. As I was filling out paperwork, I asked the boisterous woman in the cube next to me who she used as her doctor. Just to clarify, this was before online reviews caught on. Anyway, I wrote down her recommendation and decided I should probably put on my big girl pants and schedule an appointment. When I arrived for my appointment, I quickly noticed this did not look like the waiting room of a general practitioner. After taking a closer look at the photographs and pamphlets lining the walls, I finally concluded that this was a practice of gynecologists. GULP. This was new territory for me.

As I waited for my name to be called, I thought about running, but curiosity got the best of me. I decided that a mature woman should know about her body. I stuck around, using the free time to send my co-worker a WTF text to thank her for her recommendation. Come to find out she had had five children in the last decade. She probably hadn't seen any other practitioner in years!

Years later, I cornered my mom about never scheduling a gyno appointment for me. Her response was that I could have scheduled it myself. I went off to college having never done my own laundry, so it seems unlikely that I would have scheduled my own doctor appointment, but moving on…

Roughly ten years after that appointment, my first pregnancy reached a point where I could no longer ignore that this growing baby was exiting my body, whether I liked it or not. I could have just thrown my hands up in the air and said, "Well, this is going to happen to me anyway; I'll just let the doctor do his thing."

Or, I could have scheduled a c-section to avoid childbirth all together, like one well-meaning woman in the online birth group I joined when I found out I was pregnant, "I scheduled the sh*t out of my c-section and would totally recommend it to a friend. When it is scheduled, there is less risk, less discomfort, and your scar may even look better."

I guess she may be right if she assumes her only options are a scheduled c-section or an emergency c-section. But it's pretty sad that she doesn't believe she can have a positive birth without the aid of major surgery. Then again, what did I know? I had never given birth before. But that kind of passiveness didn't sit right with me. After thirty-three years of avoiding the topic, I decided the healthiest route would be to try to learn about the evidence surrounding birth options and then make my choices accordingly.

Your Team Matters

I began to devour birth stories like they were warm, free cookies in a hotel lobby. It became clear from the birth stories and evidence-based practice I read about that the people I surrounded myself with at my birth would play an important role in how my birth unfolded. I wanted a fellow woman by my side who believed in a woman's ability to birth and had routinely witnessed minimal intervention births. A coach that could talk sense into me when I was crumbling. A partner in crime to experience the highs and lows with me. An advocate guiding me to the finish line.

Childbirth is not something women get a practice run at. At some point, the mountain will seem too high to climb. In your moments of weakness, you will need support. Plan what that will look like ahead of time.

Many health care providers think they are helping women by solving for pain management, which can be fantastic! But I hope they also realize that childbirth doesn't have to be easy or pain free to be positive. Take the birth stories in this book, for example. A woman can fully experience birth and come out on the other side with a positive story to tell. How is that possible, you may wonder? It is because she felt safe and supported, and got to be fully in control of her body as she helped her baby enter this world.

At thirty-two weeks, I switched care providers from an OB-GYN to a midwife. Traditionally, a midwife is more likely to suggest minimal intervention options, believing in the body's ability to give birth without assistance, whereas OB-GYNs are trained in how to use medical interventions to guide childbirth and perform surgery routinely. Most have had limited exposure to what birth looks like when the laboring woman is in the driver's seat, and the OB-GYN and their team are not orchestrating the event.

I immediately noticed a difference in the structure of the appointments. My appointments consisted of caring for my growing body and baby in a noninvasive way and also focused on preparing my mind for childbirth. When we discussed labor, there were far fewer rules or expectations about how things had to progress. It was about letting my baby and body do their job, and my midwife would be there to support me through it all. My midwife would ask me questions to establish where my head was at, similar to a therapy session. She understood that my mind would play an important part in my experience and perception of the birth process. As I prepared for birth, she asked me questions, then listened as I rattled through my fears and self-doubts. During my care visits for the second birth, she routinely asked how I felt about having to go through birth again. She encouraged me when I was having trouble remembering how strong and capable I was. Instead of offering an "out," she offered an ear, which can be just as powerful.

The care providers who you surround yourself with during your pregnancy and during your labor will profoundly impact your experience. Don't underestimate this part of the equation. Your team matters. Don't be afraid to switch providers. If you decide to birth in a hospital, ask if they have an approved midwife who delivers there who you can see for your appointments leading up to delivery. Ask if they have doulas (birth companions who are not medically trained in delivery) available during labor, or look into hiring your own. Ask your husband, or whoever you plan to have in the delivery room, to attend some of your prenatal visits with you. They are part of your team, and you do not want to be making introductions between contractions.

You need someone in your corner who regularly sees birth without major intervention. If they haven't experienced it, it will truly be difficult for them to believe it is possible. As a doula, Staci regularly witnesses birth. She emphasizes the value of having the right team around you—one that believes in your body's ability before invasive interventions. "I have seen women totally change their care course when a doctor comes in and starts making strong worded suggestions."

Once a baby starts growing in your belly, there is no doubt it will be exiting. We must acknowledge that each intervention does not stand alone. The subtly profound classic picture book *If You Give a Mouse a Cookie* illustrates this concept well. Each decision you make during labor is part of a chain reaction. It is important that you understand why certain interventions are offered and also what you are gaining and giving up when you accept them. You need to be aware of the path you are putting yourself on before you are laboring at 2:00 a.m. and an opiniated nurse is pushing you toward interventions that never crossed your mind. Unfortunately, it happens way more often than you would think. You are put in an awkward spot when they tell you it is totally routine (because it is in their world), but in this chapter you'll see that the research doesn't support that these interventions are always necessary or in your best interests.

As a country, our cesarean rate has skyrocketed to an alarming rate. In 2016, the Center for Disease Control (CDC) reported that 31.9% of deliveries end with a cesarean. It is important to note that this is actually down slightly from the all-time reported high of 32.9% in 2009, yet clearly, we have a very long way to go. Ladies (and gentlemen), this means that almost one in three women are now incapable of healthily birthing their own babies. Do you really believe that? I call bullsh*t.

While a c-section may be a necessary ending, it is also major surgery and should be seen as such. Our care providers should be setting us on a path to avoid a cesarean from the beginning, through mental preparation, as well as labor best practices. Unfortunately, the care in this country most often shoots a pregnant woman in the foot and then expects her to run a marathon. We flood her head with doubt and then take away some of her most basic needs—mobility and sustenance —and then expect her to do the most physical thing she has ever endured.

You Deserve Better Birth Practices

Thankfully, we are at a birth tipping point. The momentum is building; women are starting to question the system, and the medical world is starting to take notice. The research in favor of minimal intervention birth techniques is rapidly growing. In fact, last year, the American College of Obstetricians and Gynecologists (ACOG) released a committee opinion titled: *Approaches to Limit Intervention During Labor and Birth*. These techniques should aide in reducing the national cesarean rate. The report concluded that, "Many common obstetric practices (including interventions) are of limited or uncertain benefit for low-risk women in spontaneous labor."

But just because the evidence is now supported by the brains of the medical birth world, until the practices of the hands of the medical birth world (the practitioners on the front lines) catch up to the evidence, you must be willing to take an overactive role in your care.

The following six evidence-based birthing techniques will help align your mind and body for the most positive childbirth experience possible. Coincidently, each of these steps are also shown to reduce your risk of an unplanned cesarean. Even if the idea of giving birth "au natural" sounds overwhelming, each time you implement one or more of these techniques, you are doing your body and your baby a huge favor by stacking the deck in favor of a positive birth experience and a reduced risk of a cesarean. For that, you should feel like a birth goddess.

Pause for a minute and really let that sink in. You are a birth goddess with the power to change your outcome for the better. It would be ludicrous not to give them a try. You are so incredibly capable.

This is the exact formula that I used to have two positive, intervention-free, hospital births in the last two years while having the peace of mind that I would happily accept interventions that were necessary and in my best interest. These six steps will help you achieve your own birth that uses only the minimal amount of intervention needed. The **M.I. Birth Method** is an evidence-based plan that makes you and your capable body Plan A, the center of the birth process; it reserves necessary medical intervention for Plan B, and it reduces your likelihood of an unplanned c-section.

Sounds pretty ideal, right?!

I'm so glad you are ready to learn more. Do yourself a favor and take a bathroom break, grab a snack, and refill your water bottle.

You are about to change the way you approach birth. Ladies, it's time you claim your superpower! The following section shares exactly how to do it. Begin on the next page when you are ready to get started.

THE SIX STEPS TO YOUR OWN MINIMAL INTERVENTION (M.I.) BIRTH

1. Believe that Your Body Was Made for Birth

Your body was literally created with childbirth in mind. Women were given the equipment to give birth, while men clearly were not. The scientific evidence is there. It is not a fact that we need to spend much time debating.

However, believing you have the equipment and believing you are capable of partnering with it to let it birth on its own are two totally different things. One is a fact, while the other is emotional and takes courage. Your mind and body are deeply connected. Be your body's best friend and partner in birth. Invest in training your mind. I don't mean that in some loopy, high-as-a-kite, disconnected from reality, hippy-dippy type of way. There are some very concrete steps you can take. They all revolve around filling your head with evidence-based education before going into labor.

This particular book was not written to teach you all the science behind the miracle of birth. I am not a doctor. And as I've confided in you, I was not always super in touch with my body. In my twenties, I felt like an awkward twelve-year old girl every time I walked in to a gynecologist's office. But because of that, I was forced to find some fantastic educational materials to prepare for birth once I was pregnant. Below is my personally recommended crash course:

During your first trimester, read *Expecting Better: Why the Conventional Pregnancy Wisdom is Wrong—and What You Really Need to Know* by Emily Oster. It shines a spotlight on each piece of birth advice women are given and uses scientific evidence to explain the "why" behind that advice. From there, you can decide which adages you wish to adhere to.

Things like how safe is it to dye your hair or eat cold cuts during pregnancy, to why they smear eye ointment on your new baby just after birth. The evidence-based advice in this book will make you feel well informed when the Starbucks barista asks you if you want decaf to go along with your baby bump instead of your regular latte. It will also give you a foundation for having informed discussions with your practitioner about which kinds of interventions you wish to allow.

Around the time of your second trimester, watch The Business of Being Born. It focuses on labors and deliveries that use minimal intervention birthing techniques. It is important to visually soak in what birth can look like when a woman is not connected to a hospital bed, is fully aware of her body, and is able to partner with it to birth her baby. This gives you another reference point for birth. It doesn't mean you have to choose to deny all interventions and birth in your living room, inhaling peppermint essential oils and gnawing on a tree branch for pain, but it will help you make more informed birth choices for the type of experience you want, and that is always the goal.

By the time the third trimester draws near, you will be ready for a lesson on your amazing body. Picking up *Ina May's Guide to Childbirth* will deliver that lesson, backed by the data of thousands of minimal intervention births that Ina's team of midwives have attended.

The other half of her book includes some amazing birth stories and was actually a large part of the inspiration for this book. It does a great job of describing what birth can look like when we support women and let their body perform its miracle. However, my beef with it is that it falls quite short of being relatable to the modern woman. Most of the births take place on a farm in rural Tennessee. While most of us aren't thrilled with the level of intervention that has been injected into birth in this country, we don't sway as far as to want a farm birth experience either. You will find the birth stories in Ina's guide very informative, but you are much more likely to find a woman you relate to in the latter pages of *this* book.

In a perfect world, I recommend taking in these resources in the order they are listed because each will open your mind up a little further. It will prepare you to take in the next level of useful birth information when you are most likely to need it.

While evidence-based information is critical, it is important to invest in your emotional education as well. An emotional education is the act of giving your mind strength through positive affirmations and stories from women who have birthed before you. This type of education is the specific intent of the stories you will read in the second half of this book.

Childbirth is not exclusively an act of rational thinking. It is highly emotional, and we cannot afford to minimize that. At some point we will end up making decisions for our bodies when we are right in the heat of labor. These decisions will either be rooted in fear or rooted in a belief that we are capable and cared for.

The evidence-based and emotional education you provide yourself with will be the vessel from which each of these next five steps flow from. I am so glad you are reading this book and making an investment in your emotional education. If you begin to believe in your body, you are already on the right track to achieve your own minimal intervention birth experience.

2. Hire a Coach

Even your very best intentions may start to waver when the eye of the birth storm is closing in around you. Your body and mind will endure physical and emotional gymnastics. It can be exhausting. You may reach a point of fear or self-doubt. And while in the midst of labor, it may feel intimidating to question a medical professional or a suggested intervention, even if it doesn't go along with your initial wishes.

As a sensible person like yourself could imagine, it is very counterproductive to leave a woman alone in a room to labor with her fears, offering medical interventions as her primary option to manage the situation. It becomes very likely that she will accept these interventions early on if she doesn't have a knowledgeable and loving advocate in the room.

It is critical to think through your support system long before you go in to labor. A coach's role during childbirth is to support your physical and emotional wishes. This person can offer support by helping you exhaust minimally invasive laboring techniques to improve the situation before suggesting a medical intervention. Someone to provide counter pressure on pain points. Someone who can suggest new labor positions that could alleviate pain. Someone who knows what childbirth looks like and can assure you that you are safe, and your body and baby are progressing well. Someone who will stay by your side during the latter half of labor.

BECAUSE YOU ARE SUPERWOMAN

Who you choose to be your coach is acutely significant. You need to think of this role like you would if you were to hire someone for weight loss, or to prepare you for your first marathon. This person will be expected to challenge you in a healthy way to reach the positive outcome that you requested. I'm sure you would choose to work with someone who had a track record of patient success. Some people assume that their spouse or nurse will provide sufficient support, but I urge you to look further.

Your spouse hasn't given birth before, nor attended many, so it is going to be difficult for them to own the situation on your behalf. Even if they seem calm on the surface, they are likely a ball of nerves underneath. They are smack in the middle of their own emotional journey and may lack the skills to "keep the calm" when their beautiful spouse is moaning and slamming her fist on the interior of the car door as they gun it to the hospital. It really isn't fair to plan to put all that responsibility on their shoulders.

On the other hand, a nurse may routinely see labor, but she can't be expected to stay by your side. She has other patients to manage and job functions to perform. Most nurses will only spend about one third of your labor in the room with you, most of which will be spent checking monitors, recording vitals, and administering interventions. Only about ten percent of their time is spent offering patients emotional, physical, or informational support. An OB-GYN may check in on you from time to time and magically appear to catch the baby, but they will spend even less time with you than the nurse.

An experienced midwife and/or doula should be able to provide the patient coaching and support you will need. Their continuous care techniques have been linked to lower cesarean rates in numerous studies. They spend extended one on one time with you through the course of labor, they routinely see birth, they are highly trained in low-risk techniques to help you cope and advance labor, and they have experience educating their patients about their options. A midwife is licensed to deliver babies. She can be paired with the patient support of a doula or act on her own.

While a doula is not licensed to deliver babies, the emotional support she provides offers incredible value. She can be paired with a midwife or used in conjunction with an OB-GYN to fill in any emotional and continuous support gaps.

Our healthcare system is slowly starting to acknowledge that professional and continuous labor support leads to fewer medical interventions. However, it will take a while before the new evidence and the routinely accepted best practices realign. Don't be afraid to request the type of care you desire, so that providers are forced to make a more concerted effort to expedite the "catch-up" process.

This step of the M.I. Birth method should take time. Finding a coach you connect with may require a few first dates before you find The One. But the time invested will be worth it. Try calling your hospital or practitioner's office to see if there are any midwives on staff or doulas that they routinely work with. You can also check out the Midwives Alliance of North America or Doula Match to find your own local options.

Don't tell yourself that you are stuck, that it is too late to switch providers. I switched from an OB-GYN to a midwife during my third trimester. I liked my OB-GYN, but I had to be honest about what the evidence showed that I needed from a coach and what my OB-GYN was experienced in providing to her patients.

Your coach is an invaluable part of your labor experience. The knowledge, love, and support you receive from them will shape your birth experience and how you feel about it. It is worth taking the time to choose wisely. It might be a while before you get a do-over.

3. Let Labor Begin on its Own Terms

Toward the end of pregnancy, it has become almost common practice to ask a woman when she plans to induce. Induction is the act of artificially kick-starting labor, meaning we are forcing our body to do something on a timeline other than its own. The CDC reports that over twenty percent of labors begin with induction, while many other reputable sources state considerably higher percentages. As a country, we have become a bit complacent toward induction, treating it as a routine intervention, but that is a dangerous stance to accept.

Some doctors, and even pregnant women, tend to love the idea of induction because it is a calculated way to start labor. Other women are just over being pregnant by the end...which is reasonable after months of discomfort and joyful antic-ipation.

But when you try to control labor in this way, you are strip-ping your body's ability to know when it is truly ready to labor. You have taken away it's opportunity to partner with you to deliver your child.

Not going into labor on your estimated due date is not a reason you must take control of the eviction process. We could all do ourselves a favor by acknowledging that a due date is not a hard expiration date. It should be seen as part art and part science, since every woman's menstrual cycle varies in length. Naturally, going into labor two weeks before or after your due date is safe and more common (when our bodies are left on their own clock) than we are lead to believe.

Don't underestimate the power you provide your own labor by practicing patience. Sorry friend, I don't like that idea just as much as you. Patience is like a modern achiever's F-bomb. I can barely sit still long enough to let my nails dry after a manicure. We don't like to slow down and just wait for things

BECAUSE YOU ARE SUPERWOMAN

to happen. We like to make things happen. Heck, most days I pride myself on that very fact. But the data has shown that induction rates have risen and fallen in accordance with our nation's cesarean trends. Inductions have been responsible for changes in fetal heart rates, infection, and contractions of the uterus that are way stronger than your body would create naturally. All of these factors lead to additional interventions being introduced into the situation. In this case, patience is a small price to pay for a M.I. Birth experience.

You have a better chance of practicing patience in the comfort of your home than you do feeling like an actual patient in the hospital. It is completely safe to stay away from the hospital until labor has progressed. Most first-time mamas head to the hospital far too early and arrive at around 3 cm dilated, which is well before reaching active labor. Your care provider will give you a guide to help you understand when it is ideal to head in. It will be something along the lines of 4-1-1 for first-time moms, contractions that are four minutes apart, one minute in duration, and consistent for one hour. If you have any questions as you labor at home, call your provider and discuss with them how you are feeling. They will let you know if there is any reason to come in sooner.

It can be very discouraging to get to the hospital too early and find out you are barely dilated. Once you are fairly certain that labor has begun, try to rest at home. As labor progresses, it will be more difficult to sleep comfortably. For most women, labor is a marathon, not a sprint. You will feel stronger, happier, and more confident about delivering your baby if you enter the hospital well-rested.

Contractions will get to a point where comfortable rest is no longer an option. It is very possible that your contractions will still not be consistent enough to rationalize racing to the hospital. In that case, it is time to throw yourself a party. Labor is here, you will soon be meeting your baby. You are doing great. Now celebrate. Eat, drink, and be merry! No really. Eat. Drink. And be merry!

Eat nourishing foods because later in the game, there may be restrictions placed on what you can eat by medical staff, or you may just not be interested in scarfing down food during heavy contractions. But remember how hangry you get on a typical Tuesday at 4:00 p.m.? Eat now. Your body will need the energy later.

Now drink, drink, DRINK!

What?! No one ever told you that the same mantra you used during your college party days would come in handy during labor? That's a shame.

You really do need to drink up so that your body stays well-hydrated. It is hard to think clearly when your brain is foggy from dehydration. Remember, your body is in the midst of performing an extremely physical act. You hydrate at the gym. Make sure you hydrate in labor.

Okay, so the 'be merry' part is a little tongue in cheek. You probably won't feel super merry at this point. But moving around will help to calm your mind and will help to let gravity move your baby down. Take a walk. Do some squats. Circle your hips on a yoga ball, or dance in the middle of the room just because you're awesome. Vacuum your whole damn house. Take another walk. You get the idea.

Be patient and believe in your body. Your baby will not stay in there forever; labor will eventually begin, Mama. And once it does, enjoy that house party! You are now one step closer to your best birth experience. Make sure to celebrate you, the guest of honor. It is time to get excited for the logic-defying magic trick your vagina is about to perform.

4. Don't Become a Passive Patient

Once you do enter the hospital or chosen birth location, it is not time to completely hand over control of your labor. You are not a patient in need of healing. Heck, you don't even n e e d to change into a hospital gown if you don't want to!

You are a laboring woman who needs care and coaching to make it through until your sweet little babe shows up to the party. There are some specific things you can do to stay active and involved in assisting your body's progression.

Electronic fetal heart-rate monitoring (EFM) was introduced in the 1970's and has since become a routine labor intervention, used in around ninety percent of births. Its claim to fame was that it would detect fetal distress and eradicate cerebral palsy.

That claim has since been debunked, but hospitals are still playing catch-up with care techniques, at our expense. ACOG's research concluded that women with low-risk pregnancies do not benefit from the routine use of continuous electronic fetal heart-rate monitoring. The current research does not indicate a decrease of cerebral palsy with the use of EFM, and "non-reassuring fetal heart tones" picked up on EFM's have become the second most common reason for first-time cesareans in the United States. Fetal heart tones can change frequently with the position of the laboring mother and are not always an indicator of true distress. While there is a benefit to monitoring, non-reassuring fetal heart tones (for a limited amount of time) may not be a sufficient reason for an immediate cesarean. Furthermore, EFM restricts your mobility by continuously attaching you to a monitor. This prevents you from finding the labor position that you find most desirable in the moment.

The good news is that there is a happy medium. You can request intermittent monitoring. The staff can temporarily connect you to the fetal monitor and then take it off after their reading is complete; this will continue at regular intervals. There are additional non-restricting, hands-on options, that have been associated with more favorable outcomes, such as the fetal handheld doppler or a fetal stethoscope. However, these require specific training to use, and as of now, traditional staff in the U.S. are not regularly receiving this kind of medical training, which means they are not likely to be offered to you—yet.

The next tether that hospitals routinely bind women with are IVs: a pole with a bag of fluid attached that flows into your body through a needle inserted in your vein. However, they have not been proven to be necessary or beneficial. ACOG now acknowledges that women don't generally require a routine, continuous drip of intravenous fluids. While it is completely safe, being attached to an IV pole will restrict your mobility and make you feel more like a patient.

Of course, as we covered earlier, fluids are really good for your body during this time. Since you are not a patient, you can self-administer these fluids without an IV. Realistically, you will be in the midst of concentrating on a number of important coping techniques. Reminding you to drink frequently may be the perfect job for a spouse or coach to assist with. If they want to reach superstar status, they will hold the cup while you drink (I recommend a large one with a flexible straw), or feed you the world's most highly regarded labor snack—aka ice chips.

Personally, I chose water infused with a little Skratch powder added. It is a concentrate that my husband and I have used while training for endurance sports. It delivers a little natural sugar and sodium to keep the body energized and hydrated for extended physical events.

If your hospital gives you a hard time about forgoing the IV, or it would just make you feel better to have it as a ready-to-go option if necessary, you can ask for a saline lock. This means they will place the IV needle in your arm but cap off the other end so you aren't actually attached to anything.

Overall, just remember, mobility is seriously your Best. Friend. Forever. You will likely desire to change positions numerous times during labor. A walk down the hall, a soak in a birthing tub or shower, circling your hips on a yoga ball, hanging on to your partner's neck to redistribute weight, or leaning over the bed to get a lower back massage. Each of these positions will make different parts of your body expand and contract. As your baby moves down and your body opens up, what felt good before might no longer "do it" for you. But if you are free to move around, you get to be an active participant and try something new.

Personally, I spent time in a variety of positions that would have been difficult or off-limits if I were attached to a fetal monitor or an IV. I wore my own clothes, so I felt more like myself. I requested intermittent monitoring so I could pace the room and later lay in a warm tub. And I chose to forgo the saline lock, which meant I literally had nothing put in my body during labor. I retained all the mobility in the world. Well…as much mobility as a super-pregnant woman can realistically achieve with a beachball where her stomach used to be.

Taking charge of specific steps to feel "normal" and maintain mobility was a much healthier game plan than being in a paper gown, on my back, hooked up to machines, feeling like a delicate little flower.

Delicate little flowers are not in control. But you are.

5. Time, Not Intervention, is Your Friend

Once you enter the hospital, it can start to feel like you are on a time-clock, and sometimes, you literally are, depending on the hospital's "best practices." But please remain calm. Often times, all your body needs is time. There is not a strict time table that your body follows during birth, so there is no reason to get discouraged or feel like your body is failing you if things don't move as fast as you (or restless care providers) would like.

The most current information from ACOG states that active labor really doesn't start until a woman dilates to six centimeters. And once there, "failure to progress" is defined as labor with ruptured membranes and routine uterine activity with no further dilatation for four to six hours. So, depending on when you enter your birth location and depending on whether your body is ready to evict that baby now or enjoy a little more cuddle time with your snuggle bunny on the inside, you probably need to pop a chill pill before assuming your body requires an intervention.

Failure to progress is actually the number one reason for unplanned cesareans in the United States. A primary reason is that most care providers are still operating on Freidman's "failure to progress" guidelines from the 1950's, which started at 4 cm dilated and said a woman with routine uterine activity should not stall in dilation for more than two hours.

ACOG's new evidence-based recommendation above supports women having more time to labor. It is slowly being adopted by care providers, but it can take years to change bad habits and mindsets that have over a sixty-year history. It is very possible that you will still need to be your own advocate and request more time to let your body do its best work.

We live in an instant gratification time in history, but our birthing bodies never got the memo. As much as we have evolved, the way we birth our babies (when left to labor without intervention), is relatively similar to how our bodies did it thousands of years ago, long before we were on some strict time schedule.

Now remember the mobility that you just protected all mama

BECAUSE YOU ARE SUPERWOMAN

bear style? Continue to make good use of it. Those walks, position changes, soaks in the tub/shower, massages, drinking fluids, etc. will help the minutes pass. When you feel like you are on the verge of becoming overwhelmed by the thought that you don't know how much longer you can hang, just promise to take labor one contraction at a time. Commit to getting through one more contraction, and then give yourself the freedom to choose if you would like an epidural.

You may be absolutely sure that you want to get an epidural, which is your prerogative. Or you may be adamantly trying to avoid an epidural, which is also your prerogative. But likely you fall in the gap somewhere in between. You think it would be pretty incredible to go completely natural, but the commitment is way too overwhelming since you won't know what you are up against until you are "in it." The good news is no matter where you fall on this spectrum, time is still your friend.

Epidurals have been shown to slow or stall labor. This could be because your body is not fully able to partner with the contractions to progress. Another possibility is that gravity is no longer assisting you along because you are laying on your back in bed. In addition to your lower half being numb, you will be attached to an IV and catheter. Mobility will truly become restricted. By delaying the epidural, you are allowing your body to move your baby further down into position to make their grand exit.

When labor isn't progressing, staff often begins recommending additional interventions to keep things moving. These interventions have been linked to increased cesarean rates. Each additional contraction you crush on your own, prior to the epidural, moves you one step closer to a minimal intervention birth.

But Mama, please hear this. An epidural does not mark a failure point. If the pain is too overwhelming, and you or your coach are not able to help you reclaim your emotions, you can actually become your own worst enemy and fight your body from progressing. The power of your mind can hold the baby in longer than necessary. Take it contraction by contraction, try not to get overwhelmed, and know that with each minute, you are that much closer to meeting your baby. First, offer your body time. Then, take a deep breath and decide what you honestly need from there.

6. When Your Body is Ready, Assume the Position

Congratulations! You made it to step number six, the grand finale. Things will be getting really exciting down south. Your cervix will eventually do you the honor of dilating to ten centimeters. Most of us have been told this is when we get to actively start pushing our baby earth-side.

Hold up. It may very well be time…but it may very well not be.

As you've probably picked up on, there is a theme to the M.I.

Birth method. I know you are seriously not going to like me when I tell you again, but patience and time are your BFF. Just because your body has reached 10 cm, your baby may still not be low enough in your pelvis to make a swift exit. If you start pushing too early, you may run out of steam. Pushing fatigue can get lumped into the "failure to progress" catch-all bucket we talked about earlier. So, you want to arm yourself to avoid that in this stage as well.

If your body has the urge to start pushing at 10 cm, by all means, enjoy that change of pace from contractions. A good care provider may even recognize that it is time for you to push based on the change in the moans/groans you are involuntarily making.

You will feel a strong amount of pressure when the time has come. Ladies. I apologize for this mental picture, but it is going to feel like you are going to deliver your baby through the back door. Listen to me, you won't. You are completely safe, but the pressure is one you won't be able to ignore. You. Will. Know. The good news is, that pressure means your body is working beautifully. Your baby is *so* close!

On the other hand, if you reach full dilation, but your body isn't experiencing the immense pressure or an involuntary urge to push, you should probably push the pause button instead of pushing out your baby. There is no need to start pushing now and try to force things along. In fact, the current recommendation to avoid unnecessary intervention is to let a woman wait one to two hours after reaching 10 cm to see if her body begins to bear down on its own (ACOG). When you and your body are working together, it speeds up the pushing phase, and helps you avoid exhaustion and feeling discouraged.

Once it is clear that your body is ready to push, it is time to assume the position. Are you picturing yourself on a bed, legs in the stir-ups, and your upper half elevated to a forty-five-degree angle? Probably. But that position has become the most commonly accepted position in the U.S. out of convenience much more so than benefit. It allows staff to easily be involved, all the medical tethers can stay in place, and women don't need assistance to achieve it when their lower half is numb. But, if you have retained mobility, the possibilities are endless!

Gravity is your amigo, and trying different positions can help open your body up. In fact, laying on your back actually makes your pelvis opening smaller than when you are in an upright position. It has also been shown to lead to more time spent in the pushing phase. Many women who are not forced to birth lying down say that they enjoy standing, squatting, leaning over the bed, or being on their hands and knees. It turns out, when not contained, we are still very primal creatures during birth.

Sure, the idea of birthing on your hands and knees may sound strange now, but if you are in a supportive space during labor, you may be surprised what your body is naturally inclined to do. Hopefully, the stories in this book will offer you some new mental images of what "normal" can look like when it is time to bear down. Hell, you probably won't want to poopoo any option to help get your baby out sooner!

(If you are wondering, yes, that was an intentionally lame poop joke to make you feel better about the possibility of pooping while pushing. Let's just get over that fear together right now. Thank you.)

Let's do a quick little review. Below is a convenient list you can use to help mentally recite the six M.I. Birth techniques as you lie in bed wide awake at 3:00 a.m. during your third trimester. You can also pack a copy in your hospital bag, because everyone needs another thing for their hospital bag—just ask Pinterest:

The Six Steps to Your Own Minimal Intervention (M.I.) Birth

1. Believe that Your Body Was Made for Birth

2. Hire a Coach

3. Let Labor Begin on its Own Terms

4. Don't Become a Passive Patient

5. Time, Not Intervention, is Your Friend

6. When Your Body is Ready, Assume the Position

I have successfully used these six steps to achieve two beautiful and empowering intervention-free births. Even though I had to fight off my own demons of self-doubt, I understood the fact that each intervention I accepted came with its own side effects.

Mentally, I planned to forgo the epidural. Not because I wanted to experience pain, but so that I had what felt like the best possible chance of making my own decisions. I would be able to wear my own clothes, I would be able to walk around and get in any position necessary to encourage my body to progress. I could soak in a tub. I could eat and drink. I could push in any position that felt right. I could feel in control, instead of being controlled.

My goal was not to feel like I was a patient. I was not damaged goods, in need of a doctor to make me better. Labor and delivery would be hard work, but my body was about to do something very powerful. I was about to produce a miracle. I wanted to be involved.

As a country, we need to stop making our biggest birth decisions based on the worst that could happen. By committing to as many of the M.I. Birth steps as you can, you have put yourself on a path to achieving your own minimal intervention birth.

BECAUSE YOU ARE SUPERWOMAN

It is time to start investing your time and energy in that possibility. You are not helpless. You are literally life-giving. You are so unbelievably capable of stacking the deck in favor of a positive birth story. You must be involved in your care decisions. You are a bad*ss birthing woman. I want to hear you roar!

In fact, I want you to start practicing now. A strong roar is incredibly powerful to help you push that baby out!

4 YOUR BIRTH STORY MATTERS

I didn't always feel comfortable channeling my inner birth goddess.

In fact, when I first started to consider that I may want a midwife instead of the OB-GYN I was seeing, I drafted up a meek little email on my practitioner's patient portal site, asking if it would be offensive to drop my doctor and start seeing the midwife—mind you, I was over thirty weeks at this point.

The patient portal boasts that it is confidential, and in my head, I somehow concluded that that meant only a nurse or assistant would see my email and advise.

I was mortified when my OB-GYN wrote back and said, "No problem. Why don't you meet with the midwife for your next appointment and see what you think?"

Ugh. If I had been more of a grown-up, I would have just asked her to her face if it was alright, but I'm not. Thankfully, it all worked out.

I saw the midwife for my next visit and instantly felt like we were a good match. Though in my head, I really leaned toward a natural birth experience, she didn't put any sort of pressure on me to commit to that. She just told me that her philosophy was to use practices that support a woman's mind and body during birth. She had routinely witnessed birth with minimal intervention or no intervention at all. She believed that each woman was capable of giving birth, and she was just there to assist in what her body already knew how to do quite well.

That was the first time I really felt like a medical professional believed in my body's natural ability to give birth.

Positive birth stories don't have to be unicorns. Reread that, and start to believe that.

I promise, they really do exist. And there are more of them out there than you realize. But there is an accepted dialogue around birth in this country. Birth is scary, painful, unnatural, should unfold in a perfect pattern, and it demands medical intervention.

That was the message I had received from society, and I accepted it. Anything less than a doctor, an epidural, and laboring on my back was venturing into hippie territory— *until I got pregnant myself.*

The more I learned, the more I felt conflicted. Everything I thought I knew about birth seemed questionable. It no longer felt like these accepted interventions were in the best interest of the woman. It felt like an intervention-free childbirth should actually be the starting point for the birth discussion, instead of the option viewed as what crazy, uneducated, poverty-stricken, or careless women choose to do.

I've had two unmediated, hospital births in the last two years. I'm here to tell you that an intervention-free birth doesn't have to be scary or crunchy.

It's unfortunate that Ina May's childbirth book is still one of the only resources being passed around on natural birth. I sincerely love that book, but a book about natural birth on a hippy commune in rural Tennessee isn't going to resonate with most women. It is not a likely starting point for someone questioning what they, a modern woman, wants for her birth experience. But once your mind is open, please read it. It is a fantastic resource!

We need to extend positive birth stories to all women, even those who are not convinced they want a totally intervention-free birth. They should know it is a realistic option. It is the most noninvasive form of childbirth possible and allows women to avoid many negative, or unnecessary, interventions. It can be very empowering. Most often, it is a healthy and safe option for the mama and her baby. And it's not some reckless, crazy act reserved for those who love self-torture. This book does not offer all the answers. It should be considered the gateway drug that leads you to crave learning more about childbirth.

I find myself questioning how our society has convinced smart women to casually agree to major surgery without strongly considering that her body is equipped for birth? Often times, it is fear that practitioners, family, and friends have instilled. Whether these individuals realize it or not, the way they talk about birth highly affects women during a time in which she is hyper-susceptible to persuasion. Pregnant women are not sure what is about to happen to them, but they have been conditioned to believe it is not good. I have read countless birth stories where a woman chose an induction or c-section just because…

- She was taught to fear that her doctor wouldn't be present if she didn't schedule the date around his work schedule.
- She was taught to fear that she was putting her baby in extreme danger if she went a day past forty weeks.
- She was taught to fear that her large baby won't fit out of her vagina.
- She was taught to fear that her lady-parts would never be presentable once a baby had been pushed out of them.
- She was taught to fear that she would be risking her and her baby's health by having a vaginal birth after a cesarean.

- She was taught to fear everything that didn't fit the box: breach births, birth of multiples, letting her body labor past the ripe old age of thirty-five.

None of these beliefs are setting women up for success. They teach us to fear birth. Medical intervention is an amazing option when needed, but it should not be the norm that women are routinely encouraged toward.

I've learned that sharing my own experiences will never be enough. But there is power in numbers. There is power in reading each of the unique birth stories that the women in this book experienced. Once we get more comfortable with examples of what birth can look like, we become less expectant of our bodies and births to fit a perfect box. We no longer have to make our decisions based on these self-limiting beliefs.

For most women, having their eyes opened to alternative birth options and believing that they are capable of achieving them are very different. All of the education in the world likely won't convince a woman that intervention-free birth may be for her. Nothing in life is completely rational: the way we eat, the way we spend, those we choose to marry, or the way we treat others. It is our feelings that play a huge role in everything we do. Birth is no different. Birth is extremely emotional.

It is the stories of women who are just like you and have achieved a minimal intervention birth that will inspire you to believe that maybe, just maybe, it is possible for you, too.

It is our job to plant the seed of belief in other women. Belief that your body is not a lemon. Belief that your birth experience can be gratifying. Belief that you have choices in your care. These are the types of things that can make all the difference in your birth experiences.

Women need to read many empowering stories to begin to change the birth monologues that society has ingrained in their minds. By sharing a collaboration of minimal intervention birth experiences, I hope you come away believing that not all childbirth is the crazy sh*t show that we been taught to fear.

The next chapters of this book seek to expose you to many types of positive minimal intervention birth experiences from some fierce women. Before you assume they all had the perfect birth scenario, spoiler alert: THEY DID NOT. All of these women had to fight the limiting beliefs in their heads to courageously move toward the type of birth they wanted.

These are not your typical birth stories. They are filled with positive and challenging examples of what birth looks and feels like when it is felt in all its glory. They are the stories from bold, educated, strong women who decided to do things differently.

- Breadwinning women who worked until the day of labor
- Women that had health issues that they overcame to birth the way they believed their body could
- Incredibly short labors (baby arrived eight minutes after arriving at the hospital)
- Very long labors that challenged the women to their core
- Many women who were scared of the pain of childbirth
- Women traveling the globe during their pregnancy
- Women fighting the dreaded back labor
- Women who had their birth choices questioned (repeatedly)
- Women who worked out and moved right up until the end of their pregnancy
- Women who went one to two weeks past their due date to let their body go into labor on its own
- Women who switched providers in the middle of their pregnancy to gain the type of support they craved
- Women who gave birth at home, in birth centers, and in hospitals…with OB-GYNs, midwives, and doulas in every birth position imaginable
- A woman who gave birth in one of the most progressive birth countries and received in-home care for almost two weeks after birth (provided by her insurance)

- A woman with a traumatizing birth experience who later went on to achieve the M.I. Birth experience she hoped for
- Even a mother pregnant with twins who was able to deliver unmedicated

These are the remarkable stories of modern day superheroes. A bunch of incredible superwomen, just like you. Enjoy the stories they have so graciously shared. They did so specifically to give YOU the power and confidence to go after the minimal intervention birth experience that you desire. A fantastic birth experience that likely strays far from everything you've been conditioned to think about birth. A positive, empowering, life-changing moment in time.

Read these stories and really let them permeate into you. Then read them again if you need to. Remember, we are trying to change your beliefs about birth, and it is going to take a lot of positive reinforcement.

From there, commit to follow the six steps for a Minimal Intervention (M.I.) Birth. By following them, you will write your own amazing story that you can spread to the next generation of powerful, bad*ss birthing women.

5 JADE'S BIRTH STORY: TAKING CONTROL OF MY HEALTH TO FIND MY INNER SUPERHERO

MEET JADE –

1. Education: Northwood University, Midland, Michigan, bachelor's in International Business and Management

2. Primary Job During Pregnancy: Regional Sales Manager for an automotive supplier

3. Age at Delivery: 34

4. Two Ways I Prepared My Mind for Birth: 1) Staying positive and visualizing a calm, beautiful, and pain-free birth, and 2) Getting past the fear surrounding birth and remembering it is natural, and my body was designed for it

5. Two Ways I Prepared My Body for Birth: 1) Staying active with yoga and walking, and 2) Seeing a functional medicine

doctor to get my body chemistry in order before getting pregnant

6. City/State of Birth: Royal Oak, Michigan

7. Location of Birth: Karmanos Natural Birth Center at Beaumont Hospital, Royal Oak

8. Delivery Date: 41 weeks + 3 days

9. Present at Birth: Husband, midwife, doula, and two hospital nurses (one for me and one for baby)

10. Did I Prefer Contractions or Pushing? Pushing, because I had breathed the baby all the way down. It was one quick and painful push, and she was out.

11. Two Resources I Recommend to Others Preparing for Birth: Hypnobirthing class and maintaining a calm and positive mindset. I did this with lavender baths, yoga, and my favorite music.

12. Have I, or Would I, Aim for Another Minimal Intervention Birth After Experiencing It? Absolutely. I would follow the same birth plan.

13. My Empowering Message to Women Considering a Minimal Intervention Birth Plan: You have Wonder Woman inside of you, I promise. You will find more strength in you than you ever dreamed you contained. You will feel like you ran a marathon, but be willing to run one hundred more just for the chance to meet this tiny little human. You can do this. Your body was built to birth. Your body knows what to do.

You just have to breathe, relax, and allow your incredible vessel to do what it already knows how to do.

Life Before Baby

I was thirty-four and married to a truly amazing man. We lived in a lovely home in a suburb of Detroit. I was a well-traveled, college graduate and Regional Sales Manager for a flourishing automotive company. I was active in my company's women's networking group and community outreach activities. We had a remarkable black Labrador that could hunt, catch a frisbee midair, and was a therapy dog to boot. We also had a cranky elderly cat and several horses. I was a busy bee and reveled in the calming power and challenge of yoga, trail riding on a warm summer day, and riding dressage (a competitive sport where one partners with a horse in the training of precise movements and development of the horse's natural athletic ability).

You're rolling your eyes, aren't you? I am very aware that my life sounds like a Lifetime movie, and I am thankful every day for my good fortune. As often as possible, I pay it forward. But life is more than select moments in an Instagram filter. I've had my challenges as well.

I had a rough accident with a horse a few years ago that took me out of work for a month, required reconstruction on eight teeth, a year and a half of vertigo, physical therapy on my hip, and surgery on my intestines. I still have no memory of the day it happened. Sadly, my husband will never forget my goldfish memory in the ER and that I didn't remember I was married. He tried to input some humor in the situation and asked if I remembered our six children. I was horrified in the moment, but looking back, I find it comical.

Recovery came with weight gain, depression, the inability to ride my horses or do yoga, and a significant increase in severity of my Interstitial Cystitis (IC) flares. IC is also called Painful Bladder Disease. Imagine someone repeatedly stabbing you with a knife in your urethra. That is what an IC flare feels like. The frequency and extreme pain of the flares led to two surgeries, which led to two superbug bacterial infections, which led to two PICC lines. Even after the infections were gone, I felt like I'd aged decades and was living in constant fatigue and pain. Hence, my daughter's birth story happened a few years later than we originally anticipated.

With only more pills being offered by two different IC specialists and continuing to feel worse and worse, I went to see a functional medicine doctor for a different approach. Functional medicine takes a whole-body approach to treatment, with the understanding that all systems are connected. It also incorporates holistic and traditional medical practices, as it focuses on the root cause versus symptom management. I truly believe this decision not only helped me get well again, but also helped me get pregnant and have a pretty ideal pregnancy overall.

When my blood test results were reviewed at the first appointment, I was shocked at how inflamed and exhausted my body was. I was the most anemic patient she'd ever seen, deficient in many vitamins, minerals, and hormones, plus an undiagnosed autoimmune disease. My imbalances were so severe, it would have been extremely difficult to get pregnant and stay pregnant. Within eight months, I was off all my IC meds, felt great, was riding and competing with horses again, and very happily pregnant.

Pregnancy

I am a true introvert, a perfectionist, a rule follower, a planner, an organizer, and constantly struggling to make everyone around me happy. I overthink everything and do exhaustive research online before making any decisions or purchases. My husband would also describe me as a little "hippy-dippy." I was a vegetarian for nineteen years, all our food in our house is organic, I'm an avid book lover and a bleeding heart. Our first dance at our wedding was to Van Morrison's "Into the Mystic," and I wear a ring every day that says, "I want to rock your gypsy soul."

We agreed to genetic testing but chose to leave the gender a surprise. Leaving a bit of mystery ended up being my favorite part of my pregnancy and gave me an extra boost of energy at the end of labor. We took many classes and read countless books. The classes put me at ease, just as lavender bath bombs do for some.

I needed some calm energy in my life early on in the pregnancy. I had accepted a promotion right before finding out I was carrying this bundle of joy. I was lucky enough to perform my old and new job at the same time, while experiencing all-day nausea for ten weeks. Whoever called it morning sickness was very wrong. In my case, it was all-day sickness. To hold off physically being sick, what worked for me was snacking or drinking something constantly and taking vitamin B-6. Why is it that "morning sickness" happens so early in the pregnancy that you can't even tell anyone? That doesn't seem fair.

So here I am, working like a dog, trying not to throw up on anyone, keeping the biggest secret of my life and with two work trips to Mexico. These are not trips to the beach, believe me. Let me paint you a picture. Ever spend three hours in a non-air-conditioned cab that smells like a middle school boys' locker room? Now, take that cab and put it in Mexico City's gridlock with a driver that speaks zero English, add in a passenger that is already on the edge of nausea in ideal conditions, and that was my trip! My high school Spanish failed me, and I was trying to mime to the driver to pull over because I was going to redecorate his interior. Yeah, not a good start to pregnancy. Luckily, it was all uphill from there. At fifteen weeks, I was finally able to hand off my old job, the nausea disappeared, and I could finally tell my secret. I felt like Wonder Woman. I suddenly loved everything about being pregnant and my growing bump.

There are a lot of important decisions to make when you're pregnant: choosing a doctor/midwife/doula team, a birth plan, a name, child care, a pediatrician, vaccinations, and figuring out all the alien-looking gear we were expected to put on a registry. As an overthinker, I worried about things like picking a biodegradable diaper, free of chemicals and dyes. I wanted a name that was simple, timeless, easy to say and spell, but looked good on a resume. I wanted a pediatrician that would honor my decision to extend my child's vaccination schedule, wouldn't over-prescribe antibiotics, and had better office hours than 10-4, three days a week. All these decisions were time-consuming but enjoyable for me.

I devoured research on things like Vitamin K shots, the necessity of vaginal exams, and delayed cord clamping. I watched movies and series like *The Business of Being Born* on my iPad while I got ready for work in the morning. I took hypno-birthing and breastfeeding classes, and watched every hypno-birthing and natural birth-related video on YouTube in existence. After all my research, I decided I wanted a birth that was more miracle and less medical.

I focused on taking care of me as well. I was the vessel for this growing being. I made time for at least five minutes of prenatal yoga daily to stretch out my lower back. I always got at least eight hours of sleep. I liberally applied coconut oil to my ever-growing belly. I monitored the local Facebook Mom2Mom sales for used baby gear and clothes to save money. I drank my daily organic "Bun in the Oven" hot tea. My husband and I took our dog, Gus to our favorite park to play Frisbee and hike each weekend, no matter the weather. I nested. I made huge pots of soup and froze half of it. I did a major frozen crock pot meal cooking session with my sister-in-law. I spent silly money in Costco on frozen organic meals. I believe the comment from my husband when I made an exceptionally large score was, "I can tell a pregnant lady went shopping."

My husband was kind and patient with me and attended all our prenatal appointments. He read scientifically based baby books, like *Brain Rules for Baby: How to Raise a Smart and Happy Child from Zero to Five* by John Medina, and *Thirty Million Words: Building a Child's Brain* by Dana Suskind. It may have been the pregnancy hormones, but I felt like I was falling more in love with him every day. He was an incredible partner through this experience, and this bad*ss mama became a complete mush ball for him. We had been through so much, and he was there with me through every speed bump. He always chooses me.

Being pregnant is a very public experience for an introvert. I had several moments of uncomfortable touching of my lower abdomen without my permission and before I was even showing. I had hundreds of conversations with co-workers and friends about wildly personal things like my "bloody show" and if I would have my "membranes stripped." It was bizarre, to say the least. On the other hand, I also felt honored that they felt comfortable sharing their personal stories and cared enough to discuss mine.

This was truly the most important job I'd ever been given. I wanted to give this child every opportunity for a healthy body and mind and a lifetime of success. It was going to start from day one in my belly. My OB-GYN has grown into a large practice and has a midwifery division that I chose to go with. They were associated with my doctor I'd been seeing for over a decade, had my complicated medical history, and aligned with both my logical mind and my hippy-dippy soul. They suggested hypnobirthing classes and delivering at the Karmanos Natural Birth Center at Royal Oak Beaumont. I was sold. They had a team of midwives, so the plan was for me to rotate my appointments with each of them, so I had some familiarity depending on who was on call when I went into labor.

Hypnobirthing was essential to the success of my birth. I grew up memorizing my mother's traumatic birth stories. My mother was four weeks late with me, induced due to placenta depletion, labored for thirty-six hours, and then I broke her back. That's a heavy emotional burden to carry. She wasn't supposed to have any more children, so you can imagine how my brother's birth went. It was certainly faster, but she lost too much blood for it to be considered anything less than life-threatening.

Hypnobirthing helped me get past these negative birth stories and not absorb anyone else's negative experiences. I gained my confidence in the statistics that my instructor gave—that 95% of births are completely normal and don't require medical intervention. Women have been doing this since the beginning of time, largely unassisted and devoid of modern medicine. Several women in the last decade have given birth unassisted while in comas. Just as my body can build this human with no help whatsoever, it can birth this baby. My job was to remain calm and keep my vessel healthy.

Animals give birth unassisted, untrained, and without someone yelling at them to push. I needed to forget my fear conditioning and the screaming cinematic births. I would birth unassisted as well, but with all the needed medical equipment and medical staff close by on the off-chance I fell in the 5% with true complications.

I also took comfort that my body type was more similar to the women on my dad's side of the family who had very positive births. My husband loved to remind me, with a sly grin on his face, that I was going to be great at this because of my family's hips. I visualized a fast and painless birth utilizing these glorious hips. I had been practicing yoga for about ten years and that gave me a solid foundation for the meditation part of hypnobirthing. You learn to relax deeply to help prevent the fear-tension-pain cycle. I wanted my child to have every psychological benefit associated with a peaceful, non-medicated introduction to this world. I would do everything in my power to protect that experience. My previous medical history taught me to confidently be my own patient advocate. All of my science-based research pushed me to not be a "good" submissive patient.

I stopped taking birth control about one year before we got pregnant to start tracking my cycles with an app on my phone and to give my uterus the chance to build a thick lining. We would end up using other methods of pregnancy prevention for a majority of that time due to my illness. Having that time to really watch my body go through natural cycles was eye-opening. I had been on birth control for over fifteen years at this point. I had no idea what my natural cycle was. This new knowledge helped me understand exactly when I actually got pregnant. So, when my original due date was March 9th, I completely agreed. When, at the second ultrasound, they changed my due date to March 2nd, my only pregnancy regret was not speaking up.

BECAUSE YOU ARE SUPERWOMAN

Due dates are estimates. They can be wrong by up to two weeks in either direction. However, when you get close to or past this estimated date, suddenly the medical community forgets this window of error. As we approached my due date, I had a negative experience with one of the midwives who leaned a little more toward the traditional medicine side. According to her, there was considerable risk associated with going even one week past my due date but no risk associated with the induction pill. It was also suggested that I have my membranes stripped, because it was a "natural" way of inducing labor. I saw red flags. I was angry. I was scared.

There was no risk in going a week past my due date if my due date was wrong. There was nothing natural about a painful procedure where someone sticks their fingers where they shouldn't be, initiating labor before my body was ready, introducing outside bacteria and potentially breaking my water. No, thank you.

My husband and I had previously decided that we wanted as few people in the delivery room as possible. It would just be the midwife and the two hospital staff nurses (one for me and one for the baby). Now, I was reconsidering. What if this particular midwife was the one on call? What if she pressured me into induction, Pitocin, and who knows what else because of her personal beliefs and verbiage like "the safety of the baby." This was NOT my birth plan. My resident calm demeanor was evaporating quickly. I reached out to the doula, Janice, who taught our hypnobirthing class. I had no

85

idea where my head would be when laboring, and I needed another female in the room with my same beliefs to advocate for me.

Keep in mind that I was at 38 weeks along, so this was a wild request. Luckily, the stars aligned. The doula validated my concerns and called a midwife friend of hers at my practice. Her early March birth had delivered three weeks early, so she agreed to support me. I immediately felt better. The new midwife moved my scheduled induction from 40 weeks + 6 days to 41 weeks + 5 days. This timing was because of a terrible rule that you can't deliver past 42 weeks at Karmanos. I stressed about this. The birth center's list of stipulations was extensive, and I had met all of them. I had the perfect uncomplicated pregnancy and had gladly agreed to labor without drugs. The idea that I might have to give up that tub and queen-sized bed because of my incorrect due date was frustrating.

I made the decision to allow the scheduled induction appointment to prevent alarm with the midwives, but I had no intention of taking that pill. I felt calmer once I made this decision. I would deliver when my body was ready, even if that meant going past the official 42-week mark and delivering in the traditional delivery area at the hospital. As long as the baby was completely healthy, it was important to me to stick to my plan. I was not uneducated on this topic. I had done far too much research and knew that when you induce labor before your body is ready, the use of Pitocin jumps, then the need of pain relief increases, and then the likelihood of c-section—you guessed it—goes up. This was not a rabbit hole I wanted to fall down.

So, as a good rule follower, I hit my due date and did the required weekly ultrasound and twice weekly non-stress test. I obsessively hydrated before my ultrasounds so there wasn't an issue with the quantity of amniotic fluid. I had a very active baby, but I brought ice water to the non-stress test to guarantee a lot of movement. I wanted no reasons to use that induction date. I was lucky, and my 40-week ultrasound estimated a 7.5-pound baby, not too big or small, still within the Karmanos requirements. I felt lucky to have access to such a center, but conflicted that so many women are deprived of the experience of Karmanos because of archaic rules based on estimates.

I declined vaginal exams. There was no benefit to me. I didn't want to introduce unnecessary bacteria into my body, and I didn't need the anxiety of knowing that I was or was not walking around dilated for weeks at a time. To bring on labor, I regularly reminded myself that I was relaxed and safe. I listened to calm music, and I worked from home after my due date. I visited with my sweet elderly horse and walked my dog a few times a day. I took long candlelit baths, rubbed Clary Sage essential oil all over my belly, and had sex with my husband. I had long conversations with the baby about how loved he/she was and how we were ready to meet him/her. I am ashamed to admit, in a weak moment, I bought a bottle of castor oil and had no clue if I had the guts to use it. At that moment, it made more sense than that dreaded induction pill.

At this point, I was getting used to being a spectacle. For over a month, I had been receiving countless text messages, phone calls, and fielded comments from co-workers that I looked like I was ready to pop. People give very forward advice to pregnant women. I had one woman who had no children tell me to induce because I didn't want to have a large baby. Call me crazy, but a large baby was the least of my worries. I knew my body would not create a baby I couldn't birth. I knew that with hypnobirthing, women around the world had given birth to babies 10 lbs. and greater with no tearing.

Everyone reacted with elevating levels of terror when I mentioned I was past my due date and out and about in the world. I knew when my correct due date was, and I knew that first-time moms deliver on average at 41 weeks + 3 days. I saw myself soothing everyone around me, and I saw the humor in that.

I chose to accept the attention positively. I had really amazing people in my life who truly cared about me and my child. We received carloads of used baby gear from friends and co-workers. The generosity was overwhelming. We wanted for nothing baby related. I felt the love, and I made sure the baby did, too.

My 41-week appointment fell on a Friday. I had my ultrasound and non-stress test, but I felt different. I had been lucky enough to not have any swelling and plenty of energy throughout my second and third trimesters. This day, my whole body ached, my legs had swelled to twice their size, and I was exhausted. My midwife, Sarah, got very excited when I told her this, and I took this as a good sign. She speculated that I would go into labor on Sunday and deliver on Monday when she was on call. I loved this plan and set in my mind that this would happen. One more weekend with my husband, a Mexican dinner out, and one last hike with my dog. Some final kisses on my horses and last-minute nesting.

Labor

Oh, the power of visualization. The midwife was right. The first contraction came at 11:40 p.m. Sunday. My two close friends whose birthdays were that day would be disappointed. It was unlikely they'd be sharing their special day unless the baby came out of me like a slip and slide. I opened my contraction app on my phone and started the timer. I was unsure if they were Braxton Hicks or real ones, so I watched them for forty minutes before waking my husband.

The first one was seventeen minutes before the second. They quickly moved to six minutes apart, five, then four. I lit some candles, turned on my music and got in the tub, with the advice of the midwife and doula that I needed to relax and get rest because it could be awhile. After only an hour, they were two minutes apart. This couldn't be, right? Labor would slow down again, I was sure. First babies are traditionally slow. I had no bloody show. My water hadn't broken. We were instructed to go to the hospital when I had contractions every five minutes for one minute for one hour straight. When contractions were every two minutes for one minute for an hour straight, I got nervous we were going to have an accidental home birth.

At 1:30 a.m. I called the midwife and doula again and asked them to meet me at the hospital. In true perfectionist fashion, my main concern was that I hadn't turned my work out-of-office on before we left the house. We got in the car and started the half hour drive to Beaumont with me directing my husband on who to call and what directions we needed to give my Dad to care for our dog and cat. He knew perfectly well how to care for our animals and who to call, but I'm sure it made me feel better to have control over something.

Ten minutes into the drive, I felt nauseous. I knew that feeling well. Luckily, there was a plastic grocery bag in the back seat, and I grabbed it just in time. That final Mexican dinner was liquified. My husband was nervous. I remember telling him that it was going to be fine and directing him to the correct entrance in between surges. We ended up going down a one-way in the huge hospital complex, which I found humor in, even in the middle of labor.

We got a great parking spot, and my husband grabbed our bags. It was a slow walk since I needed to stop every two minutes to press the timer on my app and breathe through the sensations. We got to a locked door because it was after hours, and a nurse, on his way to work, kindly let us in. We took the elevator up to the 3rd floor. The kind check-in woman gave me a piece of gum to get the sick taste out of my mouth, and I slowly answered their questions between deep breaths and leaning over the desk with my head down on my forearm. I wouldn't describe the contractions as painful. They were strong feelings, but manageable. They were certainly a pressure unlike anything I had felt before, but I was confident that I could handle them. I continued to remind myself to relax my shoulders and not fight the sensations. I needed to let them flow through me.

They pulled a wheel chair around and took me to triage. They rolled a curtain around my hospital bed. I slowly changed into my blue cotton labor dress that I had carefully picked out. It had buttons down the back like a hospital gown and straps that folded down for the first skin to skin contact and breastfeeding. Little did I know, I would only be wearing this pretty little dress for all of twenty minutes. I declined the vaginal exam from the triage nurse and asked for my midwife, Barb, to check me. It was very important to me to be checked infrequently and by the same person. I didn't need some new person checking me halfway through labor with the determination that I had failure to progress and needed medical intervention. I'm sure you're seeing a trend with my birth plan here? The theme is: everyone needs to get out of the way and let my body do what it instinctively knows how to do!

Barb stuck her head in the curtain to say hello and put her gloves on. She excitedly announced that I was 7-8 cm dilated with a hearty "good job, and it looks like we're seeing a little bit of bloody show right now!" This immediately alarmed the triage nurse, who referred to me as "girl."

"Girl, I know you're having a contraction, but we need to do this or you're going to have this baby here in triage."

The poor nursing student from Oakland University struggled nervously to hold the Doppler in place on my belly for the required twenty minutes while I insisted on sitting up on the side of the bed. We managed it all after she finally listened to me on where to put the monitor to get my baby's heart rate. They wheeled me into my beautiful Karmanos delivery room. My dream was becoming reality.

In the moment, I had no interest in digging out my bathing suit, and proceeded to strip down and slowly step into the tub. I was introduced to my nurses and to all of their amusement stated, "I do apologize, I didn't plan on being naked for all this."

My eyes closed, and I barely opened them again until I met my baby nine hours later. I had no concept of time. I labored in the tub for a while but couldn't find a comfortable position, so I moved to the bed.

Bless my doula's heart. She put on some soft music and came and went from my side as I needed her. The wild thing was that I didn't know what I needed, but she did. I could not get enough ice water. Cool wash clothes on my forehead felt like heaven. Her encouraging statements that everything I was doing was right and beautiful were like magic words. My husband was right along with her. He rubbed where I needed to be rubbed. He put straws in my mouth to drink. He held my shaking legs as I tried several laboring positions and supported my exhausted body to and from the bathroom. Hell, this gorgeous, patient, and brilliant man even helped me wipe my ass. There were a lot of comments from me along the lines of "so much poop," with apologies.

At 7:00 a.m., there was a shift change, and Sarah arrived. This was my favorite midwife, and I was glad to know she was there. I remember one moment when she was lying on the bed next to me, caressing me softly and whispering words of encouragement.

Oh, my shaking legs. It felt like they were constantly going to give out, but you know, they never did. I was so tired, but astonishingly I was able to labor lying down for a while with the peanut ball between my legs. I got brief moments of slumber between each surge. That was the reboot of energy I needed. The nursing team apparently got a kick out of my infrequent but clear direction on what I needed, exactly when I needed it. Particularly, my very detailed directions on leg massaging I gave to my husband when I labored in this side-lying position.

I reminded myself over and over that no one was hurting me. This was my body creating these sensations. My body would not do anything that I couldn't handle. With each contraction, I visualized the waves crashing on the beach in Florida, where we vacationed when I was a child. I focused on relaxing my shoulders and making my body limp.

I vaguely remember one or two more dilation checks and the intermittent Doppler checks of my baby's heart rate. I honestly did not see the nurses' faces until after I delivered. I kept my focus and stayed in the moment. After triage, I was never aware of where I was in the labor process. This made the updates my husband owed our family lack detail—which I heard many frustrating comments about later on. I was so grateful to not know how much further we had to go. I didn't know if we had been there an hour or a day, and my doula kept me focused on getting through each moment. It was exactly what I needed. My shaking legs wouldn't have been able to hear that after six hours of labor, I had six more to go. She gave me cotton pads with peppermint essential oil to invigorate me and bites of applesauce to sustain me.

It became more obvious to me, and everyone in the room, that we were getting close to the end by the audible animal noises I was making, something along the lines of a moose mating call. They came out of me without my permission and couldn't be held back. My instinct was completely in control, and those were the noises my body needed to move through each wave. My doula complimented and guided me through the sounds and asked me to lower the tone which miracu-lously helped to lower the intensity.

My doula and husband coaxed me into new positions using the peanut and birth balls. My final position was something my husband had anticipated. I was going to birth like a horse. I was up on the bed, on my hands and knees over a birth ball with my ass in the air.

My doula felt I needed to give the baby more room to progress. She suggested I put one of my feet flat on the bed to open up my pelvis. So one leg stayed kneeling while the other leg moved in to a squat.

I felt a full feeling that I can only describe as something like the largest poop in my life. My doula directed me to start my birth breathing. In hypnobirthing, there is no pushing; we use the J breath, which travels towards your tailbone in a J shape. During pregnancy, you practice this breath when you're on the toilet. I started my J breathing, and I could actually feel the slight movement downward of my baby. Like two steps forward, one step back, over and over again. Later on, my husband told me that the nurses had never witnessed a birth like this before and were in awe of my self-control and the gentle and slow progress of the baby's decent.

I could feel something wet and sac-like dangling out of me. I was not alarmed, though, because no one else was. The room continued to remain quiet and calm. I remember being filled with anticipation on meeting this little person and finding out if it was a boy or a girl. The pressure increased again and bordered on pain. My baby's head emerged and I heard someone say that there was a full head of hair. Joy filled me. I was told later that my child's head emerged with the caul, meaning her head was birthed enclosed in the water sack membranes, which ruptured as the rest of her body came out. This was an extremely rare type of birth.

My doula asked me to hold the breath at the end of each surge throughout this last stage of labor, and the steps backward stopped. We were only moving forward now, and I pulled the energy all the way from my toes to complete this journey. My loudest wild animal noise yet escaped me, and I felt a moment of pain that I welcomed without fear and with absolute pleasure. My husband caught our child and announced that it was a girl.

Somehow, I was on my back, leaning against the headboard. They handed me my daughter. Fairly quickly, they took her away. The delayed cord clamping was no longer the priority.

The midwife told my husband to cut the cord, and they began to manhandle my daughter over a cart at the end of the bed. They didn't like her purple color and were working to correct it quickly. Soon enough, it was decided she was okay, and she was back in my arms. I remember whispering and cooing to her how loved she was and how we had been waiting so long for her.

There was some massaging of my belly, and a large, soft object slid out of me. It was the placenta. The midwife calmly told me that she was uncomfortable with the amount of blood I was losing and asked if they could give me a shot of Pitocin. I agreed if she felt it was absolutely necessary. The Pitocin didn't work. My bladder was extremely full, and she felt that may be behind the extra blood. I agreed to be catheterized, and the blood flow decreased immediately.

My daughter had entered this world with her arm up by her head, and I hadn't avoided tearing. I needed a couple of stitches. There was a small sting of the Lidocaine needle and the slight tugging of being stitched. Nothing through this process was done without my knowledge or consent.

Those first few moments as a family were bliss. I remember, in the background, the medical team was cleaning up and heading out of the room. Without saying the name aloud, I told my husband I thought our favorite name fit her well, and he agreed.

The doula magically wrapped things up and ordered me what

would be the best veggie burger I had ever tasted. She made sure we had everything we needed before giving the three of us alone time. My daughter was beautiful and perfect, and I couldn't help but realize the miracle of creating her with my husband in those moments.

We invited our parents to come to the hospital to meet their grandchild. They joined us in the room, and I spoke her name out loud for the first time, gasping for breath between my tears. It was a happy visit.

I had a beautiful birth and had successfully accomplished my birth plan. The rest of our experience at Beaumont was amazing, too. The staff was incredible. We had adorable newborn photos taken and chose to stay another day to monitor our daughter's jaundice levels and make sure we had a strong start to breastfeeding. Early that first night, as my husband slept next to me, I remember being awake with nothing but pure adrenaline watching her breathe through the clear walls of the bassinet with complete wonder. I was in love.

Although she looked like a mini-me, she had my husband's appetite, and the jaundice quickly passed. The next few weeks, we transitioned from her partying all night and sleeping all day to a somewhat normal schedule. We entertained countless guests gifting plenty of pink clothing. I had support from my husband, mother, and a close friend so that I was not alone for the first two weeks, and we had meals from friends and family delivered daily. It was a weird feeling not minding the lack of sleep and the scabbed nipples. She was incredible, and I would do anything to take care of her every waking need. I think she sucked me in with that unmistakable baby smell. She's three weeks old as I write this, and I catch myself sniffing her constantly.

I feel like I've joined a new sisterhood—the mom club. You really can't understand until you've gone through it. I have no doubt that my husband will never be the same, but he did not carry and birth our child, and therefore, cannot totally understand my experience. Pregnancy and birth are transformational. I would do it a hundred times again for the chance to meet my daughter. I will follow the same birth plan for any future children. I completely understand, and respect, why a woman would choose to avoid the intense feelings of labor and get an epidural. I also appreciate why someone would choose to birth in the privacy of their own home. My comfort zone was a natural birth in that birth center with my husband, doula, and midwife. Birth is primal, and you need to be in a place where you feel secure with people you trust. I urge you to really consider what your safe place looks like and not to allow those around you, especially those negative storytellers, to take your perfect birth story away from you.

6 SARAH'S BIRTH STORIES: YOUR CARE CAN BE PERSONAL

MEET SARAH –

1. Education: associate's degree from Gogebic Community College

2. Primary Job During Pregnancy: Owner/Operator of Greenleaf of Madeline LLC (lawn care and landscaping on Madeline Island), and an EMT and Assistant Ambulance Director for Madeline Island Ambulance Service

3. Age at Delivery: 29 and 33

4. Two Ways I Prepared My Mind for Birth: I tried to prepare my mind for birth by repeating positive mantras throughout both my pregnancies, such as, "My body was made to give birth." I continually reminded myself of my own strength, and

I tried to limit any negative thoughts and only focused on positive affirmations.

5. Two Ways I Prepared My Body for Birth: Physically, I walked and remained active during both pregnancies to prepare myself for birth. I also ate nutritious and healthy foods.

6. City/State of Birth: Ashland, WI for both

7. Location of Birth: Ashland Birth Center for both

8. Delivery Date: Baby one: 40 weeks + 4 days, Baby two: 39 weeks + 6 days

9. Present at Birth: Two midwives and my husband for both

10. Did I Prefer Contractions or Pushing? Baby one: Pushing was the easy part, Baby two: Pushing was the hard part

11. Two Resources I Recommend to Others: 1) *Ina May's Guide to Childbirth*, and 2) I would suggest contacting your local birth center and speaking with a midwife. My midwives guided me through the whole experience and answered any and all questions.

12. Have I, or Would I, Aim for Another Minimal Intervention Birth After Experiencing It? Yes, natural (intervention-free) childbirth is the only birth game-plan for me.

13. My Empowering Message to Women Considering a Minimal Intervention Birth Plan: Natural childbirth is an incredible feeling. What women can accomplish is truly

remarkable. Once you learn what your body is capable of, there really are no longer any limits.

Birth One

A very large part of my first baby's birth was where we live. My husband and I live on Madeline Island. It is part of the Apostle Islands and located in Lake Superior, northern Wisconsin. It is a beautiful place to live, however, it makes transportation to and from the mainland in the winter months a little tricky. My baby was due on December 4th.

BECAUSE YOU ARE SUPERWOMAN

My first choice was to have a home birth, because I truly believe it is a loving and natural place to begin the process of welcoming your child into the world and becoming a mother. However, because we live on an island, we decided to have our baby at a birth center located on the mainland. We felt more comfortable knowing that if we needed any extra medical attention, we didn't have a lake to cross. The Ashland Birth Center is a free-standing birth center that requires a twenty-minute ferry ride and forty-minute drive for us to reach. We felt comfortable with this, especially since this was our first child.

Around my due date, there was a large winter storm. My husband, Ben, and I stayed on the mainland for two nights waiting out the weather in case I went into labor. The storm passed and still no baby, so we went back to our home on the island. After waiting for what felt like an eternity, my water broke on December 7th. I called my midwives right away, and they instructed me to get on a ferry. Because things were moving so slowly (I was having no contractions), we took our time and prepared for a 6:00 p.m. ferry to the mainland.

When we arrived at the dock, we were surprised to see the island crew tying up the ferry boat for the night after a very long and frigid day. We were mistaken in thinking there would be a 6 p.m. ferry. The exhausted crew thought they were done for the evening, until they saw us. They recognized our vehicle as we approached and knew they would need to take one more trip that night. They quickly guided our car

103

onto the ferry. Several inches of snow were on the ground at this time, and during the ride across, the wind blew heavy waves of icy water over the boat deck. One of the crew members checked on us several times to make sure I wasn't "having a baby on the boat."

When we reached the other side, the boat ramp would not go down. It was frozen stuck in the upright position. We watched our deckhand friend begin to scurry back and forth frantically trying to get the boat ramp to lower. Eventually he climbed over the corner of the ferry and slid down to the landing. He ran across the parking lot. He returned with a blowtorch and sledge hammer in hand. I then watched Ben and the deckhand take turns between blowtorch and hammer, loosening the ice enough to lower the ramp. At one point, I contemplated getting out of our car to help, but ultimately decided against it. Eventually, the ice thawed, and we could begin our mainland birthing adventure.

Because I wasn't having contractions and my birth fluid was a clear color, my midwives felt comfortable with me waiting to come in. Instead, we stayed at a hotel down the street. I spent that night trying my best to rest, but it was impossible with so much excitement and anticipation building up. I had very mild cramps throughout the night which felt like period cramps. I remember thinking that if these were labor pains, then this whole birth thing would be easy. Wow, I was wrong!

The next morning around 11:00 a.m., we casually arrived at the birth center. Because my water broke, it was now time to get things moving as to not let too much time go by without birthing the baby. I believe this is because the state mandates how long a midwife has to deliver the baby at the birth center after a woman's water breaks.

For the next several hours, I did whatever my midwives suggested. I used an electric breast pump, which helps stimulate the uterus, and in turn, begin the labor process. It was the most foreign and uncomfortable machine I had ever come across. I hated it. I did not realize that it was only the beginning of a very long season of life where my breasts had new responsibilities (hello, breastfeeding). I drank specific tea and rocked on a birthing ball, all things intended to get the birthing process rolling. Eventually, we were instructed to try to nap.

During the nap, my water broke again. I was told that the first 'break' was most likely a very small tear in the outer amniotic sac. This break was larger and much more fluid came out. At this point, the laboring process had begun.

The birth center is an old beautiful house that has been transformed into a space for mothers and babies. My midwives, Savi and Dana, are two of the most caring women I have ever met. They will be lifelong friends of mine. I spent the next few hours walking around the house, up and down the stairs, while having contractions. My husband was with me. I remember being surprised at how strong the contractions got. I leaned over onto furniture as they came and tried to explain to Ben what they felt like. My midwives actually left us alone in the house to labor, knowing it would be a while before anything happened. This made the experience more intimate with my spouse.

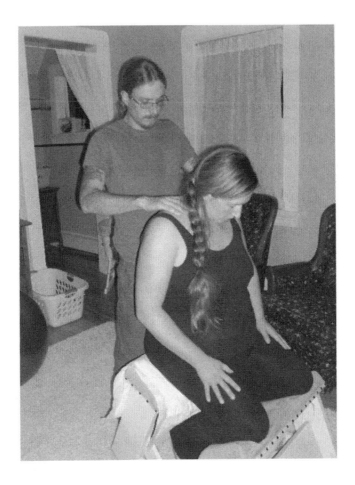

After several hours, my contractions began to get unbearable. At that point, my midwives decided to check my cervix. I remember feeling so relieved, thinking this meant I was nearing the end. The process of checking my cervix was one of the most uncomfortable parts, which I was not prepared for. After my midwife told me that I was only at 3 cm, I started to break down. I remember thinking that it was too late to go to the hospital and receive drugs! Why had I done this to myself?! After expressing my doubt out loud, I was assured that I would have a baby in my arms in about six hours. Six hours! There was no way I could do this for six more hours! I began to curse the videos of natural childbirth I had watched where women have orgasms during birth or birth a baby unassisted standing up in their living room. In the moment, I felt like they had given me a false sense of confidence. I was angry!

However, things began to move much more quickly. For a while, I was leaning over the bed hanging on to my midwife. She stayed there with me for a while. I was unable to really talk or move. It was all in an effort to get through the contractions. Because I am twice her size, I worried about pulling her across the room with my superhuman laboring strength. Luckily, that didn't happen. During this time, the midwives began filling up a birthing tub.

Suddenly, I felt an enormous amount of pressure fall toward my bottom. I hadn't realized it, but my body had gone from 3 cm to 10 cm dilated in less than an hour and a half! I was instructed to push, and I did so while standing up and leaning over a bed. The birthing tub was beside me, still filling. I pushed for what seemed like an instant, and our baby came out.

I was flooded with relief. The baby was out. As they lifted her to my arms, I saw that it was a girl. Winter Ever Schram was born at 10:12 p.m. on December 8th.

Our little family spent that night at the birth center, snuggly tucked into a warm bed. Our midwives slept close by, downstairs, ready if we needed anything. We took Winter home the next day…back on the ferry to our island home.

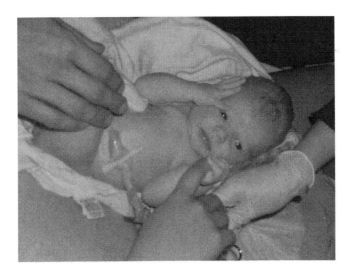

Birth Two

Like the birth of our first child, our location played a huge role in the birth of our second child. This time around, I was due on March 8th. We had a particularly cold winter that year and because of that, the ferries that normally go back and forth to the mainland were shut down, unable to break through the thick ice.

When conditions are just right and temperatures are cold enough, the lake freezes enough for us to drive from the island to the mainland on top of the ice. The ice that year was nearly two and a half feet thick, plenty thick enough to support our vehicles. If the ice road was open when I went into labor, it meant that I could simply drive across and head to my local birth center when ready. When the ice begins to melt and conditions are no longer safe to drive, islanders take a wind sled across (similar to a large, covered hover boat). I did not have to worry about a ferry or wind sled for transportation while the ice road was open.

Thus began my obsession with the weather for at least a month before I was due. I checked the temperatures for the week each morning, monitored the wind, and scowled at the sun when I felt she was showing her face too often. If my precious ice road melted, I would need to stay on the mainland and wait it out for the baby. I was not going to take a wind sled across Lake Superior while in labor if I could help it.

Because we had such an amazing experience at our local birth center the first time around, it was a no-brainer to have our second child there as well. We had now known our midwives for four years and felt even more comfortable being in their care. They seemed just as excited as we were for the addition to our family, and the chance to be a part of it. Our daughter,

Winter, went with us to most of the prenatal checks and visited with the women who had helped bring her into this world. It was truly special for all of us.

As my due date approached, I felt extremely anxious and nervous. I was much more nervous the second time around, probably because I knew what was coming. The blissful ignorance of my first pregnancy was gone, and now I remembered the intense physical transformation my body was soon to endure. I was ashamed to admit my fears, not only to myself but to my husband and midwives. I felt I should have been more confident. I knew my body could birth a child, yet I was still very scared. Toward the end of the pregnancy, I finally shared my feelings and felt much better for doing so. They were normal, and they were mine. After letting them out, I could focus my energy more on what I needed to do to prepare both mentally and physically. I read the birth stories from *Ina May's Guide to Childbirth*, trying to put myself in the shoes of the strong women who had conquered birth and hoping to get in the right frame of mind for when it would be my turn. I gave myself positive mantras to repeat. I was undecided on their effectiveness, but I was willing to try anything to keep my mind in the right place.

A couple of days before my due date, a large snow storm was predicted to hit our area. The impending weather would make it difficult to cross the ice road and travel to the birth center. Because of this, we decided to head over and stay in a hotel for the night just in case I were to go into labor. As the night of the supposed storm approached, it became evident that the snow was going to miss us. We went anyway so we could enjoy a date night on the mainland, probably our last one for some time. Our daughter was dropped off at her grandparent's house not far from our hotel destination, and we set off for a kid-free evening.

After an early dinner, all we wanted to do was relax and rest. We enjoyed television shows that weren't geared toward a toddler and settled in for an uneventful evening.

At some point during the night, I woke up thinking I had peed my pants. At this stage in the pregnancy, this was a very likely possibility. I got up to check…and the 'pee' kept on coming. While in the bathroom, I could tell that my water had broken. Yes! My water broke while I was literally five minutes away from the birth center. We had our bags packed and ready. Our daughter was safe with relatives. I couldn't believe our luck, especially since I had been seriously worrying about the whole process for at least a month!

I checked the clock. It was 5:00 a.m. I woke Ben and told him what was happening. I think he was as shocked and excited as I was. I then hopped in the shower to try and calm my nerves while this process started. While showering, I definitely noticed that I was already having contractions. This labor progression was very different from the first time around. The contractions also seemed fairly close together, but I told myself I was imagining it and tried to prepare myself for a long laboring process.

We called one of the midwives around 6:00 a.m. to let her know what was happening. She was already at the birth center with another mom who was close to giving birth. She told me they would begin getting my room ready and to call again when my contractions were stronger and closer together.

Very soon after I hung up the phone, I found myself leaning over the bed breathing through a fairly strong contraction. Just two minutes later, I was doing it again. Could this really be happening? Were the contractions really this strong or was it in my head, I wondered. Hesitantly, I called the birth center back and sheepishly explained that I thought the contractions were strong and only a few minutes apart. I was told to come right over.

We arrived at the birth center (6:45 a.m.) and went up to the room where our daughter was born four years prior. I began to cry. All of a sudden, I was hit with the reality that another baby was about to join our family. I remembered all the sweet memories we had made in that room with our first child. I felt completely at home and comfortable.

Suddenly, the nostalgia wore off! I instantly dropped to my knees as the force of a contraction bore down on me. I remained down on my hands and knees. My midwife came to check on me and could tell right away that my body was already working hard.

As each contraction came, I began a low hum. I had remembered reading somewhere that if you hummed in a low tone it helped you get through the intensity, so I did it. I think it really helped. At the very least, it was something for me to focus on.

The plan for this birth was to try the birthing tub, just like I planned last time. The tub was being filled and I had a magic vision in my head that the water would take my laboring pains away. I held on to that belief with each contraction. Soon, I would be in the tub, smiling while pushing my baby into a blissful love bath.

I continued to hum and wait for that moment. Eventually, I was told I could get in the tub. I was overjoyed and carefully made my way off the floor and into the tub. Much to my surprise, I wasn't comfortable sitting in the tub. Instead I stayed on my knees, leaning over the inflatable material that made up the side of the tub.

Shortly afterward, I was told I could begin to push but would have to exit the tub. My bottom was not fully submerged and therefore it was not safe to birth in the water. I exited the tub and climbed onto the bed with some enthusiasm. I was incredibly happy that I was now able to push. This meant that the end was near! I continued with the hands and knees position on the bed. Then I tried lifting my hands up onto the headboard.

My first baby had shot out in what seemed like an instant, and I was expecting that again. I was in for a bit of a shock when I pushed with all my strength and nothing came out. Instead, I felt an intense pressure and pain that I tried to run away from as far and as fast as I could. I could no longer hum but could only scream in an uncontrolled high pitch.

I felt like a giant brick wall was directly in front of me, blocking my path. It seemed insurmountable. Eventually, I realized there was nowhere else to go other than into the pain and began to push my baby out. My husband and midwife, who was more of a friend, were there to catch him. They quickly placed him in my arms, and I once again felt that familiar flood of relief.

As we lay there looking at our freshly born baby boy, I asked what time it was. Someone replied, "9:09am."

From start to finish, the process had taken just four short hours. Sawyer Spring Schram was born on March 6th.

We stayed in the blissful bubble of that room for most of the day while getting to know the newest member of our family. We joked, ate, and napped into the afternoon. When we felt ready to leave, we packed up our sweet boy. After picking up our daughter, our newly formed family of four crossed over the ice and headed home for the evening.

BECAUSE YOU ARE SUPERWOMAN

7 HOLLIE'S BIRTH STORIES: I KEPT TRYING FOR THE BIRTH EXPERIENCE I WANTED

MEET HOLLIE –

1. Education: Biola University, bachelor's in Psychology, minor in Bible; UCI, paralegal certificate; San Jose State University, master's in Library and Information Science

2. Primary Job During Pregnancy: Co-Owner of a small family business; Administrative Manager and stay-at-home mom during birth two and three

3. Age at Delivery: Baby One: 33, Baby Two: 35, Baby Three: 37

4. Two Ways I Prepared My Mind for Birth: Baby One: 1) Went to a birthing class offered by the hospital, and 2) Talked to my mom and cousin who had both had numerous natural births. Baby Two: 1) Re-read class materials from first birth,

and 2) Read other books/articles online. Baby Three: 1) Took a Hypnobabies class and practiced, practiced, practiced, and 2) meditated on positive affirmations, Bible verses, and prayer.

5. Two Ways I Prepared My Body for Birth: Baby One: 1) Kept exercising/walking up until I gave birth, and 2) Practiced what I learned in birthing class. Baby Two: 1) I also kept up with the walking until the end, but didn't do much else since I figured I did it once, and I knew what to expect. Baby Three: 1) Took the Hypnobabies class and visualized what I wanted to happen physically, and 2) We practiced each stage and what I would do, including birthing positions and speed.

6. City/State of Birth: All three births were in Irvine, CA.

7. Location of Birth: All three births were at the Kaiser Permanente Irvine Medical Center.

8. Delivery Date: Baby One was 40 weeks + 4 days; Baby Two was 41 weeks + 3 days; Baby Three was 41 weeks + 6 days

9. Present at Birth: Baby One: doctor, nurses, and nurses from the NICU (in case they were needed), husband, mom, and sister. Baby Two: doctor, nurses, and nurses from NICU, husband, mom, and sister. Baby Three: midwife and nurses, husband, mom, and sister.

10. Did I Prefer Contractions or Pushing? Pushing for all three.

11. Two Resources I Recommend to Others: 1) Hypnobabies!

2) Put together an ideal birth plan with decisions and procedures you want to make in case it doesn't go according to plan —research all the choices you get and your rights on what you can say no to and what are truly your options in those tough situations.

12. Have You/Would You Aim for Another Minimal Intervention Birth After Experiencing It? Definitely! At the age of 40, I am aiming for another minimal intervention birth with my 4th.

13. My Empowering Message to Women Considering a Minimal Intervention Birth Plan: Natural birth is nothing to be afraid of. It is intense and scary at times, but it is also the way we get to see just how strong and capable our bodies are. You also get to see just how strong your mind is. More important than the physical preparation is the mental preparation; anyone can do it if they set their mind to it. There can't be any space for other options. Being fully informed and prepared for the what-ifs is different from thinking about them too much. Think it through, get the answers you need to any questions, then write it all down, taking no more than a day or two. Then put those decisions aside and focus all your mental energy on the positive and empowering truth that you can do it. Don't let previous trauma or fears stop you from having a birth that is safe and natural. Conception, pregnancy, and birth are all miracles. When it happens, it is a gift to be cherished and not taken for granted. After two and a half years of infertility and a first pregnancy that ended in

laparoscopic surgery due to an ectopic pregnancy, my husband and I know something of the pain, loss, and fear felt when it doesn't happen so easily. Right at the moment I accepted that we may not have any children, we found out we were pregnant with our rainbow baby. And the rest is history. We are so very blessed as women when we get to participate so intimately in the miracle of life as God designed. No matter how the birth story turns out, there is a Superwoman in all of us.

It was my third birthing experience when I finally got an epidural free, intervention-free, all-natural birth. But my story begins with the memories of my first two children being

Baby One:

I was four days late with my first baby, and they sent me to the hospital for monitoring because he wasn't moving as much as I had expected. The monitors showed his heartbeat kept decelerating, so I was admitted for an induction. I had heard negative things about Pitocin, so I opted to have my water broken instead to try to begin labor. I felt (at the time) this was more natural, and I really wanted to have a limited intervention birth. My water was broken around 11:00 p.m., and the contractions were manageable until they weren't. I thought I was prepared enough through the birth class I took, the books I read, and talking to other moms, but I had no idea about the intensity I would feel.

My mom had experienced three unmedicated births. Had she been there with me when my pain got to the worst point (which was almost the end, I now know), I think I would have gone the whole way without the epidural. She would have encouraged me to hang on, but she hadn't arrived yet. My husband had no idea what to do when I screamed the first time. Bless his heart, he just wanted to take my pain away, so he advocated for the epidural. Looking back, I wish the doctor would have said that I was too close to the end to get the epidural—I was 9.5 cm by the time it was administered, around 5 a.m. It slowed my labor down a bit and when it came time to push (about 6:30 a.m.), I was still too numb which made it difficult to feel how well or how poorly I was pushing. Though I enjoyed pushing, the doctor was frustrated with me and ended up needing to use the vacuum to pull my son out of me. He was born at 7:30 a.m., with a cord wrapped around his neck. Thank God, he was alright, with no long-term side effects. I simply had a second-degree tear from the vacuum, and all thoughts and memories of the birth were quickly forgotten as soon as I held my son.

Baby Two:

Eighteen months later, to the day, my second baby arrived ten days past my due date. By this time, I had just turned thirty-five, so I was classified as having an advanced maternal age, and my doctor was watching me closely. I went in for a checkup on Sunday at 12:00 p.m. and was told my placenta was getting old, and I would have to stay at the hospital to be induced. This time, I chose Pitocin because I didn't want them to break my water to begin labor like last time. I didn't want to take those risks this time. But this decision turned out to be worse than I imagined. They kept raising my dose until I was at the highest level possible, and I stayed there with the most intense contractions for over sixteen hours. Without being able to eat or drink anything but water and being stuck on my back in the bed, I was at a complete disadvantage and totally lacked control of what was happening to me. I finally accepted the epidural when I couldn't stop shaking and even my mom could see how distressed I was. When she said to take it, I knew what I was going through was really bad. I was exhausted and my poor baby was going through intense contractions on the inside, sunny-side-up to boot. I finally got some rest for about four hours as my body continued to work on getting her ready to exit.

It was finally around 9:30 a.m. when the doctor told me it was time to push if I wanted. I was ready for this experience to end, so I started pushing. This time around, it was even more difficult than it had been with my son. My daughter was still sunny-side-up and seemed to be stuck. I pushed countless times, for over three hours. She would not come out. The doctor finally said she would have to use the vacuum (ahh, not again!) because she was too far down to perform a c-section. Feeling like I didn't have much choice, I agreed. She went through seven pulls with the vacuum; the max they do is ten. Born at 1:57 p.m., she was taken to the NICU as soon as she arrived, and I couldn't hold her or nurse her for three hours. We both had fevers and needed tending to. I also had a third-degree tear and needed lots of stitches. We have pictures of her in her incubator with a big red mark on her head before anyone could even hold her. It was a highly traumatic experience that took me a long time to process. I began healing from this event when I started preparing for my third, but I didn't fully come to terms with it until I did some grief therapy for PTSD, for this and other experiences in my past.

Baby Three:

By the time I was pregnant for a third time, I knew with all my heart I had to make some different preparations. Mentally, I needed to be stronger and go into this next birth with confidence that my body could do exactly what God designed it to do. My mom had three drug-free births; I knew I could have one, too. I reached out on social media for tips from friends and was directed to Hypnobabies. It was the positive affirmation I needed to support the belief that I was able to push this child out without any intervention. There was a lot of visualization and practicing relaxation as well as hypnosis—the kind some people have to use when they are allergic to anesthesia. It was great! My baby kept doing flips until I was 39 weeks pregnant, and I had to use the hypnotherapy to turn her into the correct position a couple of times. My doctor was amazed I could turn her *at all*, let alone *more than once*, using the power of my mind (and a lot of prayer). So, I had the support of my husband, my mom, my sister, my hypnotherapy, and my Believe essential oil (Balsam Fir, Coriander, Bergamot, Frankincense, Blue Spruce, Ylang Ylang, and Geranium) meant to calm and empower the spirit to promote positive action. I also had my very own pink and white polka-dotted gown to wear while giving birth at the hospital. It was a visual reminder to myself and those in the room that I was taking charge of my experience and in command of the decisions I would be making for me and my baby. We printed out our birth preferences form for the nurses (decisions we had made about how we wanted our baby treated, e.g. waiting to cut the cord, waiting to bathe, breastfeeding only, etc.), and created signs for our request to keep a dim and quiet delivery room. We were all ready for the big day.

About twelve days past my due date, I went in for a check-up and was once again told that I would not be leaving the hospital. I was devastated. They wanted to induce yet again. This was not part of my birth plan. I told them I wanted to go straight to a c-section right then because I was not going to go through either of my past two experiences. But the doctor there at the time said I was a great candidate to at least try it naturally, and she had a third option for inducing—Cytotec.

My husband and I prayed about it, and I thought, what do I really want? I wanted a natural birth more than anything. I wanted the safest and most beneficial birth possible. I also knew that by having an epidural, I would not have any feeling when it came to pushing. The last time, I had a third-degree tear, and recovering from that took as long as recovering from a c-section. I wanted to feel my body push and be 100% engaged in birthing this baby. I thought of my baby and I as a team, working together, and I wanted to experience everything I could from it. So, my husband and I agreed that an epidural-free birth would be Plan A.

I took my first dose of Cytotec at 2:45 p.m., and my second dose at 7:00 p.m. By 11:55 p.m., I was 5.5 cm dilated and 100% effaced. It had been a steady progression of birth waves (contractions) and so much more relaxed than either of my first two births. The hypnotherapy was working, I had my birthing ball, my encouragement song going ("Overcomer" by Mandisa), and I was not afraid. I knew I could make it all the way; I was not going under without a fight. My birthing waves started getting much more intense after midnight, and it was hard to move, so I laid on my side in the bed just as I had visualized so many times before. At some point, the same doctor who suggested Cytotec came in.

Up until that point, I was being cared for by the midwives who the hospital keeps on call for natural births. You can request one when you get to the hospital, and they can be used until you accept advanced medical care.

The doctor warned me about the baby's heartbeat. If it dropped again, she wanted to intervene. I could hardly focus on her because I was using my energy to try and let go of the current pain, but I remember thinking, "Are you crazy, lady? This baby is coming sooner than you think; there will be no time for any interventions. Please, leave. I'm trying to focus right now."

After she left, the midwife said she was not as concerned as the doctor; everything looked fine. My water broke shortly after, around one in the morning, and within ten minutes, I let out the loudest scream of my life. I probably scared every other woman who could hear me. I knew it was time to push. I felt the urge, and my body started doing it on its own. I had great control over how I pushed and for how long. It's possible I pooped the bed, but I took the feeling as a sign that I was pushing correctly. It felt good. I liked that I could finally control something that was happening, and it was what I had most looked forward to doing. It was the shortest part but the best part. Just five minutes later, at 1:20 a.m., our little girl arrived. The midwife put her directly on my chest, just as I requested. I got to cut the cord and nurse her right away.

When the doctor came back later, she said she was proud of me for laboring naturally. I thanked her for encouraging me to try. I got the birth I wanted, thanks to her confidence in me. I found out later that she was hoping to have a VBAC, so I hope she was encouraged by me as well to fight for what she wanted. It felt so good to know she had witnessed my entire experience and saw that it could be done even after a traumatic birth experience. Every moment was worth it, and the fact that I got to give birth to my third in the same room where my second was born was the cherry on top. The whole experience felt redeeming. I was truly the woman from the song that I sang in my head so many times—an overcomer.

I am now pregnant with our fourth child, and I am hoping this time I get to go in to labor without being induced. I've told my kids that my tummy is just too warm and comfy, so no one wants to leave it any earlier than they have to. I will be telling this baby that I don't want to kick him or her out before the right time, but please do it on your own. Maybe this will be my compliant child. Ha-ha! Regardless of what happens, I know that preparation is key for me. Anything is possible if I put my mind to it. Our bodies were built for this; our minds can be trained for it. The pain of childbirth is good pain, for good purposes. I realize I am privileged; I get to partner with my child and go through this amazing, primal rite of passage to life. I am so thankful I get to be part of this miracle that science can't ever fully explain or control. And I am a testimony that even after less than ideal birth experiences, anyone can empower herself and prepare for a different outcome.

8 MARTHA'S BIRTH STORIES: YOUR BIRTH TEAM PLAYS A VITAL ROLE IN HOW YOU FEEL ABOUT YOUR EXPERIENCE

MEET MARTHA –

1. Education: UC Santa Barbara, bachelor's of Sociology

2. Primary Job During Pregnancy: Brand Development Manager, Retail/CPG Promotions

3. Age at Delivery: Baby One: 31, Baby Two: 32

4. Two Ways I Prepared My Mind for Birth: Believing that my body was capable of giving birth, then clearly knowing that I wanted to avoid drugs that could have possible side effects.

5. Two Ways I Prepared My Body for Birth: Chiropractic visits and vitamins

6. City/State of Birth: Newport Beach, CA

7. Location of Birth: Hospital

8. Delivery Date: Baby one: 40 weeks, Baby two: 41 weeks

9. Present at Birth: OB-GYN, nurses, family

10. Did I Prefer Contractions or Pushing? Pushing

11. Two Resources I Recommend to Others Preparing for Birth: A positive mindset and a good chiropractor

12. Have I, or Would I, Aim for Another Minimal Intervention Birth After Experiencing It? Yes

13. My Empowering Message to Women Considering a Minimal Intervention Birth Plan: It is an absolute miracle to create another human being. Your body is capable of growing life and delivering naturally, should you choose. Also, your husband/partner is your biggest support during this process. Make sure they update all nurses/doctors with your birth plan, ask questions, and have them speak up for you. Things can change very quickly and get overlooked.

I had the ability to labor my two children naturally. For that I am forever grateful. This was a decision that I had made years before I was pregnant, and I knew in my heart that everything would go as planned. I really wanted to avoid any harmful side effects from medication and help my body heal naturally and quickly after childbirth.

I delivered my children at the hospital without interventions and received much love and support from my family. The best part is, my wonderful sister videotaped each birth. I have the opportunity to relive this incredible miracle with my children every year on their birthday.

Birth One: My Baby Boy in Twenty-Three Hours

I just knew my son would be born on his due date, and he was. The eve before his birth, I enjoyed a dinner outing with my husband and mother-in-law; southern comfort food and a glass of red wine. Although I hadn't experienced any contractions, I told them that this baby would be coming and that my body just felt different.

On our way home, I began having light contractions, which felt like small cramps toward the front of my belly. Once home, I paced around the kitchen island, counting the minutes between contractions, and got a few hours of sleep. My plan was to stay home as long as possible and wait long enough to be ready to be admitted to the hospital.

Although I preferred the idea of a midwifery center or water birth at home, my husband and I decided to birth in a hospital should any complications arise. We were happy with the prenatal care we received. I had shared my birth plan with my doctor, and he seemed genuinely supportive.

When the contractions got to be five minutes apart, I woke my husband. I was calm and very excited to get to the hospital. We arrived at 6:30 a.m. A copy of my birth plan was handed to the nurses and staff, and although I had no intention of using medications, they convinced me to have my arm prepped in case anything changed.

My family was beyond anything I could have asked for that day. There was good music, encouraging conversation, relaxing back rubs, and support as I walked the hall and balanced on a yoga ball. They were even breathing with me during the contractions! Their positive energy got me through it all.

The contractions were very sharp, and I had stopped dilating around 6 cm. In order to progress the labor, my water was broken. I was very nervous to do this because Nurse Courtney had assured me that the contractions would come stronger and faster, and I wasn't sure that I would be able to handle it.

Control was key. Breathing was incredibly important and vital for getting me through the hardest of contractions. I was very hot during the last few hours and had the AC turned up and a cold towel on my head. The room was lightly lit, quiet, and all I had to focus on was to push past the most intense "ring of fire" and control my urge to push to avoid tearing. It took two hours of pushing, and twenty-three hours of total labor to meet the sweetest little seven-pound boy, born at 10:47 p.m.

My husband, parents, sisters, aunt, uncle, grandma, and mother-in-law were in the room to witness my son Charlie's birth. It was a day of firsts for everyone in the room.

Our baby was the first grandchild and nephew in my family. It was also the first birth my sisters, aunt, and uncle had attended. Although it was never my intention to have a large audience, it was an amazing experience to feel so cared for and loved all day. The on-call doctor and nurses were absolutely wonder- ful, and I can't thank them enough for coaching me through it all.

Once Charlie was placed in my arms, all the pain that I had endured was gone. The only feeling left was that of love and pure joy that my baby had been born...safe, without unnecessary stress on my baby, and exactly how I had hoped it would be.

Birth Two: My Baby Girl in Sixteen Hours

My baby girl was a week late, and I was okay with it. I wanted her to come on her own time and loved being pregnant, just as I did the first time around. For ten months, she was all mine. Only I could hold her and feel her move. She would be our last child, so I wanted to hold on to this feeling for as long as she'd let me.

A couple weeks before she was born, I was excited, but extremely nervous to experience the labor process again. After my first experience, all I hoped for was a quick labor. I knew I still wanted to deliver naturally; I knew I could do it. Everyone reassured me that the second child would come faster. She did, but it still took sixteen hours.

My mother, sister, and husband helped during my daughter Rosie's birth. I was able to walk around, use a squatting bar, a yoga ball, and listen to music. My water did not break on its own. When they said they would need to break it, my heart sank because I knew of the intense contractions that would follow.

Overall, the on-call delivery doctor and nurse had a totally different bedside manner from my first experience. They weren't calming and did not give me a heads up of what was to come, especially when they would check me. It was a lot more painful. The mood in the room was cold and bright. Although my support system was there, I had hoped my experience would be more comforting all around. If I were to do it again, I would exercise more throughout my pregnancy to make labor easier, and possibly quicker. And I would consider using a birthing center with a tub. I think this would have created a better birth atmosphere for my body to labor in.

My beautiful 9 lb. baby girl was born after thirty minutes of pushing. We were all surprised at how big she was. After the delivery, she wasn't breathing well and was given oxygen to get her lungs working properly. Rosie became alert right away, opening her eyes and grabbing onto the oxygen tube. When they placed her in my arms, she latched onto me very easily and began eating. I tore naturally about an inch and did not need any pain medication afterwards in recovery. I am grateful to have delivered vaginally and was very surprised at how quickly my body was able to recuperate.

Breastfeeding went so much better the second time around. I was able to produce enough milk and breastfed Rosie for eighteen months. What a joy it was to have such a happy, easy-going baby girl.

9 STEPHANIE'S BIRTH STORY: "TYPE A" HAS THREE EPIDURAL-FREE INDUCTIONS

MEET STEPHANIE –

1. Education: Northwood University, bachelor's of business administration in Marketing/Management, associate's in Accounting/Advertising

2. Primary Job During Pregnancy: Materials Manager

3. Age at Delivery: 30, 32, and 34

4. Two Ways I Prepared My Mind for Birth: My only plan was to come home with a healthy baby, and I preferred not to have drugs so I could be alert.

5. Two Ways I Prepared My Body for Birth: I used a chiropractor and stretching.

6. City/State of Birth: Rocky River, OH

7. Location of Birth: Hospital

8. Delivery Date: 41, 39, and 38 weeks

9. Present at Birth: Spouse, OB-GYN, and nurse

10. Did I Prefer Contractions or Pushing? I guess contractions...I pushed very little with all my births.

11. Two Resources I Recommend to Others Preparing for Birth: *Scripture Lullabies: Hidden in My Heart* CD, vol. 1 and 2

12. Have I, or Would I, Aim for Another Minimal Intervention Birth After Experiencing It? Yes, especially since I have accomplished it now.

13. My Empowering Message to Women Considering a Minimal Intervention Birth Plan: Remember that there is purpose in the pain. With each contraction, envision the baby moving down the birth canal or your cervix dilating.

Baby One

I am a planner and a control freak.

When I was pregnant with my first child, Paisley, we were often told by friends (and strangers), "You need a birth plan. Make sure your providers know how YOU expect your delivery to go." But being a planner and a control freak, I knew if my delivery didn't go exactly to plan, it would not be a good scene.

So, instead, my plan was to be flexible. I planned to leave the hospital with a healthy baby. I knew I preferred not to use any drugs because I didn't like the idea of being drowsy and missing details of those first few hours after birth. It was a valid concern because of the way my body had handled medication in the past. I woke up three days after having my wisdom teeth out and had no idea how I got home to my third-floor apartment.

But even though I preferred to forgo an epidural, I never classified my plan as a "natural birth." My mother had three c-sections. I remember her being almost offended when someone said they wanted a "natural birth." She would tell them that there was nothing unnatural about having a baby, be it via c-section, with medicine, or without medicine. It was all birth to her. And she was right. I needed to decide what was best for my own situation.

My best friend had told me about a lullaby CD she listened to during her pregnancy. She is a big believer in ministry to babies in the womb, since they can hear and feel everything. The lullaby CD was supposed to help calm the baby. So, we bought it and listened to it every night. I never had issues sleeping. It was like the music put Paisley to sleep in my warm cocoon when I wanted to sleep. It actually worked for all three of my babies. The music was so calming, we decided to bring it to the hospital with us.

Prior to pregnancy, I had high blood pressure readings, so I was flagged high risk. This meant weekly stress tests/appointments.

Interestingly enough, from the day I knew I was pregnant

to today, I have not had another high blood pressure reading.

Because I was classified as high risk, at my forty-week appointment, we scheduled my induction. This started the comments from well-meaning family and friends that induction had a certain c-section outcome. We decided to stay focused on our plan of leaving the hospital with a healthy baby.

At the time, I was working for a world-renowned auto parts manufacturer as a materials manager. My position was pretty demanding. I decided to work up until 4:00 p.m. on the day we were to be at the hospital at 7:00 p.m. We ran out for a quick dinner and then over to the hospital. We were scheduled to start Pitocin in the morning, but they wanted us there the night before for Dinoprostone. Luckily, I had questioned my doctor about eating, so I was allowed to eat breakfast. We started Pitocin around 10:00 a.m. and then waited...

I was blessed to be in a hospital that believes one nurse for each first-time mom, so someone was always in the room with us, which helped keep us calm. Also, listening and singing along to the lullaby CD helped immensely. Because of the Pitocin, baby and I both had to be on monitors, but I was able to move around still and spent time on the ball and in the rocking chair.

...

By 4:00 p.m., I hadn't progressed very far, and I was getting

BECAUSE YOU ARE SUPERWOMAN

tired, so the nurses suggested a shot of Toradol, a nonsteroidal pain reliever. That let me relax, and then I started to progress nicely. I was very appreciative that the staff offered an alternative to an epidural since I had shared my intentions with them when I entered the hospital. It made me feel as if we were working together.

Transition really started to take place around 7:00 p.m. as the nursing staff was doing their shift change. The new nurse came in to check me, and she got very busy setting up the room for delivery. Soon after, I started to feel the urge to push. My nurse called for assistance, and Josh remembers everyone being pretty calm because they figured I was a first-time mom, and they had time until the nurse shouted, "No epi!" The energy in the room quickly shifted. Because I didn't have an epidural to slow my labor down, they knew things were going to happen fast if I was feeling the urge to push!

Because I had been a scheduled induction, my doctor was on duty, and the nurse told me that I was close but that Dr. Parker wanted to be there and was on her way. During the next wave of contractions, I assured the nurse that during the next set of contractions, this baby was coming with or without Dr. Parker. Right then, she walked in the room and joked with us, "What are you waiting for?"

Paisley delivered in three very intense but very quick pushes. I remember the joy and hysterics of wanting my baby. She was quickly given to me and was a natural at latching on.

While I was in the hospital, I felt like a superstar. My active delivery was just three hours. I became a bit of a hospital celebrity. All the nurses kept stopping by to tell me how amazing the delivery was for a first-time mom.

We were able to go home in less than twenty-four hours.

Birth Two

When I was pregnant with my second daughter, Riley, I remembered the pain that I would face during childbirth, but I also felt reassured knowing from my experience that it was only temporary, and my body was fully capable. We prepared for our second baby very similarly to the way we had prepared the first time. We purchased the second edition of the lullaby CD and listened to it while she grew in my belly. We were scheduled for another induction at thirty-nine weeks, honestly, so that Dr. Parker could be at the delivery. But I was still deliberate about delivering without an epidural so I could be fully in control of my body.

This time, we were able to skip the Dinoprostone and arrived at the hospital at 6:00 a.m. for induction. Our pastor met us there, and we started the day with a prayer for delivery and for the baby.

The day progressed about the same, except this time we were pros—kidding, of course. We watched the monitor and gauged how I was doing. Pitocin started around 10:00 a.m.

Sometime in the midmorning, I did have a shot of Nubain. Once again, that relaxed me, and I was able to progress. Riley was a fast and furious delivery. I went through transition very rapidly. Dr. Parker was able to make it to the room this time, but Riley came before they could reposition the bed to lift the stirrups. By 3:25 p.m. she arrived, ready to take on the world.

Riley was my most difficult baby. She cried for the first twenty-four hours. It was emotionally exhausting. We later found out that she was lactose intolerant. After I changed my diet, it got a bit better.

We were able to go home in less than twenty-four hours.

Birth Three

Since my first two pregnancies and births were positive experiences, I didn't wish to change much. With my third child, Cailey, we purchased the third addition of the lullaby CD and listened during my pregnancy.

I had started using essential oils, and we studied to incorporate those into our delivery "plan". I use plan lightly because it was still the same—to leave the hospital with a healthy baby. But I would be lying if I didn't admit I had confidence I could do it "natural" given my history.

We were induced at 40 weeks with Cailey, for the same reason as we had chosen to before; I really wanted my doctor present. She knew me, and she knew the way my body had delivered in the past. I knew I could handle the strength of the induced contractions. I had done it twice before.

We went to the hospital. Our pastor was there again to pray with us. When we were getting settled in the room, panic set in because the hospital had removed all CD players. *How was I going to listen to my lullaby music?* While I lost it, calling everyone I could think of, Josh went online and purchased a download. The calm resumed.

The Pitocin began to induce labor. After that, I remember using a lot of Clary Sage Essential Oils. It has been shown to stimulate hormones and progress labor. By early evening, I asked the house doctor for a shot of something, just to relax. I remembered that during my first two deliveries the shot let me release tension so I could ride the pain and relax.

BECAUSE YOU ARE SUPERWOMAN

I was told no, I was too close to delivery and that we didn't want to introduce any risk to the baby. So, of course, I asked for Dr. Parker. I wanted to hear from her that I wasn't allowed anything.

Dr. Parker came in and agreed with the other doctor. I was crying, but she reminded me that it was almost over, and I was strong enough to continue without it. Looking back, she was right. I was in pain, but a big part of wanting the shot was that I was anxious about what was to come. Once the shot was no longer an option, I found other ways to cope.

They offered to check me, and I was told I was at 7 cm. I got out of bed to stand to find comfort. I had one contraction, peed all over the floor (my water had previously been broken), and felt the baby coming. I told the nurse, who suggested I get back into bed, and she would check me again. I think she was trying to pacify me but was surprised when she checked and saw Cailey's head was already crowning. She told me not to push, which I clearly remember telling her I wasn't. Then to our surprise, Cailey fell out onto the bed. I remember being very thankful I had gotten back in bed!

Dr. Parker was called. When she walked in the room, she told me she knew I was close but thought she had time to check her other patients. Josh joked with her that we got to pay her to deliver my placenta.

Cailey was a content baby, and we both recovered quickly.

145

Unfortunately, we tested positive for Strep B and had to stay in the hospital for forty-eight hours. I know as a mother of three under four years I should have embraced the extra time away, but I felt we would get more peace and rest at home than in the hospital. I was happy to finally head home to join my new party of five.

10 MEGHAN'S BIRTH STORY: FIND YOUR SUPPORT TEAM SO YOU CAN DO GREAT THINGS

MEET MEGHAN –

1. Education: Grand Valley State, Art Education

2. Primary Job During Pregnancy: Middle School Art Teacher

3. Age at Delivery: 31

4. Two Ways I Prepared My Mind for Birth: I had this disk of positive affirmations that I listened to on the way to work every morning. I got it from my Hypnobirth teacher. I also listened to my Hypnobirth "meditations" every night as I fell asleep. I printed out little inspiring mantras and quotes, and I put them on my bathroom mirror. I also talked to friends who spoke positively about birth, especially those who had natural births.

5. Two Ways I Prepared My Body for Birth: I've always been

into healthy eating and exercise (running, yoga, CC skiing, and hiking). I just promised myself to continue these practices but also to listen to my body. A few months in, running wasn't doing it for me. I took a break from running and focused more on hiking often and yoga. I continued to eat healthy, but I definitely ate more red meat than ever. I usually eat red meat a few times a year. I am not a big meat eater. While pregnant, I ate it a few times a week. I also craved juice all the time, which was unusual. I usually avoid drinking juice since it is basically just liquid sugar but while pregnant I gravitated to it.

I also sat on a yoga ball at work instead of a chair. This helped with posture and strength during pregnancy.

6. City/State of Birth: Sandy, UT

7. Location of Birth: Altaview Hospital

8. Delivery Date: 41 weeks + 6 days

9. Present at Birth: Midwife, nurse, and husband

10. Did I Prefer Contractions or Pushing? Pushing

11. Two Resources I Recommend to Others Preparing for Birth: Hypnobirth class, prenatal yoga. You are likely to find a good support system with these groups, too.

12. Have I, or Would I, Aim for Another Minimal Intervention Birth After Experiencing It? Yes, but I am only having one child (not because of the birth, though)!

13. My Empowering Message to Women Considering a

Minimal Intervention Birth Plan: Women have been giving birth since the beginning of time. Your body knows how to do this. Just like it knows how to eat when it is hungry, sleep when it is tired. This is what we were made to do. Trust your body. Trust the process. And then find supportive people to surround yourself with who also believe this. My favorite saying that really sealed the deal for me when deciding to go natural was this, "The power and intensity of your contractions cannot be stronger than you, because they are you." - Unknown

The coined term "natural birth" always sounded so funny to me. Why do we have to define birth as "natural?" It seems redundant. Something women are designed for is the most natural thing in the world! But because fewer and fewer women have let their bodies birth on their own, we have forgotten how natural birth should be for our bodies.

Take for instance, something that is already natural, like apples. If we went to the grocery store and saw a new sign for "natural apples," we would question what they were doing to all those other apples to make them not natural? If we need a term like "natural birth," it raises the question, what has been done to the rest of birth to make it not natural?

Don't get me wrong, western medicine is great when necessary. But why start by messing with an amazing design? Our bodies are built to get it right. And we are fortunate because we live in an age where medical intervention is a good second option. Even before I was pregnant, I knew that I wanted to give birth with as few medical interventions as possible. So, when I did become pregnant, I decided on a "natural birth plan," *naturally*.

Because I was a middle school art teacher, I hoped to have the baby near summer break so that I could spend some extra time with my new baby. After a couple months of trying, we celebrated when the pregnancy test results were positive. I scheduled my first appointment with my OB-GYN. From there, I met with my OB-GYN for the standard appointments. I was healthy, the baby was healthy, and I felt fairly good!

I started to formulate my "birth plan" so that my OB-GYN would know I wanted as few medical interventions as possible, while keeping my, and my baby's, health a top priority. I had the full support of my husband, friends, and family when it came to this plan. Even when I mentioned it to friends and family who gave birth using any and all medical interventions (necessary or not), they still gave me a resounding "Good for you!" or "I bet I could have gone natural. I just didn't know that was an option!" Things were going great...*mostly*.

When I presented my "natural birth plan" to my OB-GYN, she seemed, for a lack of a better word, underwhelmed. She kind of just shrugged it off, barely even looking at it with me. I left her office after my twenty-week visit feeling a bit underwhelmed with her, to be honest. I knew I needed to find someone else to help me deliver my baby. It's not that my OB-GYN was unsupportive, but she was not *SUPER* supportive. I went home that day and started researching other doctors. Not to sound hippy-dippy, but I just wasn't getting the right vibe from my current doctor. I needed someone different.

What luck! In the same hospital where my OB-GYN was, I found out that there was a group of midwives! I knew a few friends who had used midwives for their births and raved about the experience. I made an appointment immediately.

This felt right. The midwives were a group of three women. I got to meet all of them on my first appointment, and one of them spent over an hour with me going over my birth plan! I was used to the OB-GYN who talked to me for five minutes! This was amazing! I now felt the support I needed. What an amazing team they were. I could still have my baby in the hospital, and the midwife rooms had a tub, which sounded amazing! They explained that whichever midwife was on call would spend the ENTIRE time with me while I was in labor. Unlike the OB-GYN who would only come in right as the baby was about to come out. The only thing the midwives didn't do was c-sections. So, if there was an emergency c-section, they would pass me along to the OB-GYN on call, since they are specifically trained for surgery.

My midwives shared with me all kinds of cool resources throughout the second half of my pregnancy to help me mentally prepare for my "natural birth." They gave me ideas on what books to read and videos to watch, and they gave me business cards for doulas and Hypnobirth coaches. These were amazing tools to have in my toolbox! How lucky I was to find them!

I ended up reading a few of their suggested books, and I also decided to do a class on Hypnobirthing. My husband and I attended a series of courses with a bunch of other expecting couples. Some of the couples were planning a "natural birth" and some were not. The Hypnobirth techniques we learned basically felt like guided meditations with an emphasis on relaxation, empowerment, and experiencing birthing "pains" as "sensations." We received MP3s of the meditations that we did during class. I listened to them every night as I was falling asleep during the latter part of my pregnancy. They were so relaxing and made it easy to get over the pregnancy discomforts of sleeping.

My "due date" was May 8. I use the phrase "due date" loosely

BECAUSE YOU ARE SUPERWOMAN

because due dates are a guesstimate! They should be viewed as a range, instead of an exact date. My mom wanted to be in town to help after the birth of her first grandchild. She flew out on May 10 and planned her return flight home on May 18, thinking she was playing it safe. My maternity leave started on May 8. Let's just say I got some quality time in with my mom before the baby came…almost two weeks later! Needless to say, my mom extended her stay.

I was perfectly content toward the end of my pregnancy. I felt no urgency to "get the baby out" or anything like that. I knew he was safe and warm in my giant belly! Why rush it? He would come when he was ready. On the twelfth day after my "due date," I was doing all the things crazy pregnant women do to keep their mind from wondering when their baby would decide to arrive. I put in a mailbox post and weeded m y garden.

Wait…is that not normal?

I never expected that when I went to the hospital later that afternoon for a routine appointment, they would make me stay!

I showed up at the hospital on the afternoon of May 18 for an appointment, so they could monitor the baby and check my blood pressure. The nurse said my blood pressure was high, and she would need to call my midwife.

"Okay," I thought naively. "My midwife will just tell me to go home and get off my feet. They know I want to go into labor naturally!"

The nurse came back a little while later. "Your midwife says she wants to induce you. You will need to stay here."

I was shocked. I guess I really just thought I could stay pregnant forever! I can laugh now about how silly this thought was, but at the time, I was like a pouting kid in the candy shop who didn't get the kind of candy I wanted. I was truly disappointed at the time, not to mention unprepared! I hadn't showered after weeding my garden, and I didn't have my overnight bag!

I called my husband who was more excited than disappointed that I was being induced. He rushed from work to the hospital. I eventually stopped my pouting once he arrived at the hospital and we settled into the room where I would give birth. My midwife arrived a short while after my husband did. She explained to me why I had to be induced at this point. Basically, my high blood pressure was not good for me or the baby. She explained that she would induce me "naturally" by inserting a balloon into me to dilate my cervix, which would hopefully induce labor. I fell asleep that night in the hospital a little crampy and crabby but also hopeful that I would be in labor soon.

The next morning, my midwife took the balloon out. Besides some mild cramping, nothing much had happened over night. I was barely dilated. "Let's break your water to move things along," she said. I sulked. That was another one of those things I was hoping that would *just happen*.

As soon as my water was broken, I felt increased pressure, but contractions were still so few and far between. It was time to bring out the big guns. My midwife said it was time for Pitocin. This was a drip that basically makes your body have contractions. I was a little worried because I knew from all my research that it was *easier* to have contractions "naturally," and Pitocin would intensify things quite a bit. My midwife and husband were awesome and assured me I could do it! I felt reassured that I could continue this without an epidural.

Hours went by; they felt like minutes and days at the same time. After the Pitocin, it all became a blur. My contractions were not super intense, but they were *there*. I spent time in the tub listening to Hypnobirth meditations for most of the afternoon with my hubby by my side.

My midwife checked in on me often. Things were still moving pretty slow, considering the Pitocin intake. My babe was just too cozy in there! I had been in labor for the whole day. Physically, I was doing fine. Mentally, it was getting old. So, when my midwife said she was going to up the Pitocin dosage to REALLY get things moving. I was like, "Let's DO THIS!"

Things got *REAL* for me the last two hours of labor. Although I had been in labor all day, I really didn't feel it was intense until about 10:00 p.m. that night. Primal instincts kicked in. No one could tell me what to do or where to go. My poor husband was there the whole time by my side but "wasn't allowed to talk" according to me. I couldn't hold still. I walked, I sat, I squatted, I laid on the floor… I did everything short of climbing up the walls. My hubby and my midwife were there the whole time, but mentally, I was miles away from them. I was in my own world.

Suddenly, I came out of my intense fog. "I need to push," I said.

"Okay!" my midwife said excitedly. I'm sure she was ready to go home at that point!

I got up on the bed, ripped off the heart rate monitor that was on my belly (I couldn't stand it anymore!) and began the process of pushing. It was late, but it wasn't midnight yet. "Let's have this baby on the nineteenth!"

Pushing was hard. I can't lie. It was so intense. My awesome midwife was such a great motivator, though. I don't remember what she said exactly, but I knew I would get through it! She propped up a mirror so I could watch my baby be born. That was a huge motivator. As soon as I saw his dark hair, I went for it! Screaming helped me push his head out. Then his shoulders were a piece of cake! My baby was born at 12:15 a.m. on May 20.

The instant I held my baby in my arms, I forgot all about the labor. It didn't matter. It didn't even matter that I was being stitched up that very moment. I was high on love and endorphins. It was the best feeling in the world. I had done it. We had done it.

Almost three years later, I still feel great about how things went. I know, just like in life, you can't control all the unexpected hiccups along the way with birth. But as long as you set your mind to something and follow your instincts, those hiccups are manageable. Based on my experience, I would recommend "natural birth" to anyone. It is an empowering and enlightening experience. You will fully experience what you and your body are capable of.

11 PAT'S BIRTH STORIES: FROM MI TO CA; THREE FANTASTIC BIRTHS WITH MY DOCTOR'S FULL SUPPORT

MEET PAT –

1. Education: Calvin College, MI and California State University (Long Beach), CA - master's degree

2. Primary Job During Pregnancy: Teacher and homemaker

3. Age at Delivery: Age 29, 32, 35

4. Two Ways I Prepared My Mind for Birth: Read books and watched a birth movie, took Lamaze class with my husband.

5. Two Ways I Prepared My Body for Birth: Exercised and practiced slow breathing.

6. City/State of Birth: Grand Rapids, MI (1 & 2) and Long Beach, CA (3)

7. Location of Birth: Hospital

8. Delivery Date: Baby one: On the due date, Baby two: 40 weeks + 3 days, Baby three: 40 weeks + 5 days

9. Present at Birth: OB-GYN, nurse, and husband

10. Did I Prefer Contractions or Pushing? Both were hard work yet rewarding.

11. Two Resources I Recommend to Others Preparing for Birth: The show *Call the Midwife* and Lamaze Classes

12. Have I, or Would I, Aim for Another Minimal Intervention Birth After Experiencing It? Definitely.

13. My Empowering Message to Women Considering a Minimal Intervention Birth: For me, a drug-free life is the best because I get to be fully present, and my recuperation was very fast. I believe you can have a similar experience with the right mental preparation and supportive care.

Birth One:

Sara's story begins in Grand Rapids, Michigan. We were so excited for the birth of our firstborn after seven years of marriage. We took the Lamaze birthing classes and watched a delivery movie. To be mentally prepared was necessary for a natural birth, which is what I really wanted for me and my daughter.

As an educator, I recognize that having a plan, or formula, is the best way to point yourself in the direction you want to go. The first ingredient of our success formula was the prep work we did. It really helped me focus and breathe through labor. The second ingredient of our success formula was the support we felt from our care provider. The wise doctor, Carl, told me that it would be fine to stay at home as long as possible. So that is what we did.

The final ingredient of our success formula was how we handled our nerves during the moment of truth. My labor started about 6:00 a.m., and I enjoyed being at home until midafternoon. My water never broke at home, but eventually, the contractions were consistent enough to head to the hospital. On the way, my husband made a quick stop to grab film for the camera. I did not appreciate his poor planning, in the moment, since he had more than nine months to prepare!

Because I managed to labor at home for so long, things escalated quickly once we arrived at the hospital. My apologies to the staff, but yelling during labor actually felt like a good release of tension. After three hours of strong labor, focused breathing, excellent coaching from my husband, forceps, and some serious screaming to release tension during the pushing phase (including some obscenities), Sara arrived at 7:23 p.m. All 7 lbs., 14 oz of her! Even during the pain, I knew it was temporary, and the epidural wasn't necessary.

We had read about the "Leboyer Method" of childbirth, which minimizes the trauma for the newborn. A warm water bath was planned ahead, and the hospital was accommodating. It was a moment of true love and wonder for my husband, as he lowered Sara into the warm water. She opened her eyes and smiled at him! It was pure and amazing. Our little miracle relaxed in the warm water. I wished I could join her.

Our first intervention-free child birth was hard but so rewarding. It was a learning experience that shaped my next two birth stories.

Birth Two:

Brian's story also begins in Grand Rapids, Michigan. Two days after my due date, mild contractions began overnight. We woke to a beautiful, spring Sunday, the kind that beckons a walk in a new nature area. When a perfect day occurs in Michigan, you take advantage of it. So, we headed out for a walk.

Soon, however, we realized we were lost! I became nervous. I may have wanted a natural birth, but that didn't mean I wanted to have my baby in nature! Praise the Lord, through hours of tense walking and mild contractions, we thankfully found our way out!

Very early the next morning, we headed to the local hospital. The wise and wonderful Doctor Carl was there waiting for us. He knew that I did not want an epidural because I did not want that type of medication flowing through me or my baby. Because I had faced labor before, the natural delivery was much easier but still a very physical commitment. Brian was smaller than my first at 7 lbs., 6 oz. My husband was, once again, a great coach.

Breastfeeding was easier on my body the second time around. My body adapted more quickly, and I was able to enjoy the early bonding experience with my baby more than the first time.

Birth Three:

Michelle's story begins in Long Beach, California. It was evening, four days past my due date, when I started having mild contractions.

In the middle of the night I woke up and went to use the restroom. My body seemed to be emptying my colon, just as it had with my first two deliveries. I decided this was it! My mother-in-law arrived at 3:00 a.m., and thankfully, we were able to drive to Memorial Hospital with little traffic. Traffic is a real concern when you live in Southern California. You don't want to go into labor during rush hour, or you may have your baby alongside the highway!

The nurses attached the fetal monitor around my belly. After watching it for a bit, they told me that I was most likely not in labor. Little did they know! My water ended up breaking while I was being monitored (4:30 a.m.), so I was staying.

I was moved to a monitoring room. While we waited for our baby to move lower in my body, we used all the natural birthing strategies that we had learned over time: breathing, pressure on pain points, using a focal point, timing the contractions, and generally trying to maintain a calm environment in the room.

My doctor, Carlos, didn't come to check on me right away because he was in delivery. We did find some amusement and ease in the fact that his name was Carlos, and our wonderful doctor in Michigan was named Carl. When he did arrive at 7:00 a.m., things were ready to go down there! I was rushed down the hall to delivery. Michelle arrived by 7:30 a.m. She was 7 lbs., 2 oz. There was laughter after her delivery when Dr. Carlos said that he would deliver all our babies! Natural child birth was worth every bit of effort with each of our children.

BECAUSE YOU ARE SUPERWOMAN

12 JOANN'S BIRTH STORY: WHAT BIRTH LOOKS LIKE IN A COUNTRY WHERE NATURAL IS THE NORM

MEET JOANN -

1. Education: Northwood University, Finance

2. Primary Job During Pregnancy: Financial Planning and Performance Manager

3. Age at Delivery: 33

4. Two Ways I Prepared My Mind for Birth: Mindful courses and took five weeks off from work pre-birth, which is a Dutch requirement

5. Two Ways I Prepared My Body for Birth: Walking, chiropractor

6. City/State of Birth: Haarlem, Netherlands

7. Location of Birth: Hospital

BECAUSE YOU ARE SUPERWOMAN

8. Delivery Date: 41 + 3 days

9. Present at Birth: midwife, nurse

10. Did I Prefer Contractions or Pushing? Pushing for twenty minutes.

11. Two Resources I Recommend to Others Preparing for Birth: Mindful meditation courses, swimming

12. Have I, or Would I, Aim for Another Minimal Intervention Birth After Experiencing It? Yes, but would plan to be in better shape before getting pregnant and do more yoga and meditation during pregnancy.

13. My Empowering Message to Women Considering a Minimal Intervention Birth Plan: Your body was made to do this. Trust in yourself and your body, and free your mind!

I moved to the Netherlands eight years ago, learned the language, lived amongst the locals, married a Dutchman, worked for a Dutch company, and bought a home. So, having a baby in the Netherlands felt natural. In fact, the word natural and baby, or birth, go hand in hand in this country.

I decided to go with the flow and do the "Dutch norm." What did that mean? To be honest, I really didn't know since this was my first baby. Looking back, there are so many firsts with your first; it can be overwhelming!

My first midwife appointment went great. She was super friendly, answered my list of questions, listened attentively to every detail of my medical history, my family's medical history, and so on. I left the appointment feeling happy, excited and comfortable with my choice. On my way out of their cozy office, I did notice the waiting room was three times fuller than when I arrived. After many more pleasant visits and baby heartbeats, I learned that the appointments were set up in fifteen-minute intervals. My first appointment at ten weeks lasted fifty minutes.

The midwife practice had four women, of which any of the four could deliver my baby. They were all very different, and I appreciated all of their styles. The frequency of appointments is similar to the States but the ultrasound "echoes" were done by a pediatrician at a different location. Visiting and chatting it up with my midwife each time felt relaxed and natural. There were no machines nor equipment in the office. Apart from the small portable baby heart monitor and blood pressure pump, all checks were done solely by their experienced hands.

I signed up for an English-speaking birth course, underwent mindful courses, added a few baby apps to my phone, read birth articles and a mindful book (*Mindful Mom-to-Be* by Lori Bregman). For the rest, I was not obsessing over the how and what of giving birth. My mindful coach (doula) was very helpful in keeping my head on straight and preparing my body. We did yoga, meditated, did mental exercises, and she went through what to expect in labor. Additionally, I had my mom and sisters drilling me with questions which I then asked at my midwife appointments. I'd like to believe that I went with the flow. In reality, I shopped and nested like crazy! I organized and re-organized the baby clothes a million times. But I did not feel stressed or nervous about the actual birth.

However, pregnancy was not all blue skies and happy thoughts as I had pain with every step I took and felt home-sick for the first time in the eight years of living abroad. As a mama-to-be, I wanted my mama!

Fast forward to thirty-six weeks, and then press slow motion, because that is what it felt like. I was grateful we were all healthy, but the impatience began. Everyone, and I mean *everyone,* told me baby will come by thirty-seven weeks; my colleagues, family and friends, chiropractor, mindful coach, people passing by…"whoa that baby is about to walk out of there!" Thank you very much. The Dutch are direct and opinionated, and this does NOT mix well with pregnancy.

One of the many differences with having a baby in the Netherlands is you are required to start your maternity leave four to six weeks prior to the due date. This was one difference that didn't sit very well with me. I wanted that extra time allotted to baby post birth.

About two weeks into my leave, at thirty-seven weeks with six mindful courses under my belt, all big purchases made, a tanned beach-ball belly and my softer demeanor (physically

BECAUSE YOU ARE SUPERWOMAN

and mentally), I started to really understand the importance of taking this time before the baby arrived. Mama and baby needed down time to prepare for their big marathon.

Okay, thanks a lot, people! It was forty weeks and no baby! I never practiced patience well, so this must've been to help prepare me for parenthood. However, I really did not want to be induced, which they do around forty-one weeks. I was walking, bouncing on my birth ball like it was my job, forced relaxation—anything and everything. I was afraid inducing would interfere with my natural birth plan. This was a valid concern because when Pitocin is used here, the birth becomes "medical" and then must be administered by a gynecologist rather than my friendly, supportive midwives. So, I was relieved when I learned they would "strip me." Stripping the membranes is a procedure where the midwife or doctor gently separates the amniotic sac from the wall of the uterus. This releases hormones that can trigger contractions. In fact, they would come to my home to do the procedure. I was at 1 cm when this was first done and, "Oww." Yes, it hurts! But I also knew that having a baby would be more uncomfortable, so I used it as practice to see how capable I was at managing pain. After the procedure, we would know within forty-eight hours if it worked. I had this done on a Monday. That Friday, I had an appointment with the hospital to plan inducement for the following Monday; come on, baby! Wednesday night, I felt irregular contractions through most of the day but tried to ignore them and not psych myself up. That evening, I was sure this was it, so I rang my midwife. She didn't think I was in labor yet, but to put me at ease, she came over to my house to check me. They try to avoid checking dilation as much as possible to avoid infection, but I insisted. Two fricken' centimeters! I called my mom crying, "This baby is never coming!" Through logic and rational thinking, my mother convinced me I was going to have a baby within a week.

The next day, another midwife came over to my house to do a second membrane sweep. I then meditated the sh*t out of going into labor by Friday to avoid the doom and looming inducement on Monday. Maybe it was all those mindful courses paying off, maybe it was the stripping, or maybe and most likely, it was our little person who was finally ready to make their way into this world, and regular contractions continued. I made it through the night and got some rest. By morning, contractions were longer and more frequent. No politeness or small talk this time when I dialed the midwife. "Hi, it's me, come here!" She didn't question me; she was on her way.

They normally encourage you to stay home in the beginning stages of labor as long as possible. However, I had Strep B, so we felt it was important I had antibiotics pumped through me before the little one made their debut. I was at 3 cm, and it was the middle of what the midwives had coined "baby season" because there were so many births happening around the same time, so finding a room at the hospital was challenging. My husband was adamant about having the passport read Haarlem or Amsterdam, so getting one of our first-choice

BECAUSE YOU ARE SUPERWOMAN

hospitals was key. Unfortunately, there were no rooms available. A third call was placed to a hospital in Beverwijk, where they had a room. No one in the United States would be familiar with the name of this neighborhood, and worse yet, Beverwijk translates into English as "Beaver Neighborhood." We must choose our battles in life and in labor. To this day, I am pleased my husband was vigilant about our birth neighborhood. He continued to press the midwives on the matter. Eventually, our midwife pulled some strings and got us into our first-choice hospital in Haarlem.

The drive to the hospital is normally ten minutes. During labor, it felt much longer; I didn't factor in all the speed bumps which exasperated the excruciating back pain I was experiencing. I was having the dreaded back contractions! I reached my room, had called my mom, but still didn't fully believe a baby was coming as I already had many "practice starts." I arrived to my room with no monitors, no machines, and I felt relieved. My husband then proceeded to lay out the ridiculous number of things I brought with me; exercise/labor ball, pillows, baby clothes, lavender oil, music speaker, dried fruit, inspirational poster of a wave with empowering quotes, etc. What stayed in the bag and at the door? My clothes and my shame.

I stripped my clothes and laid in the fetal position. From that point on, my eyes remained closed for most of the time. Back contractions, seriously?! Why me?! I wanted to snort that lavender oil to increase relaxation. According to my midwife,

175

once she checked me, I needed to get out of my head. My labor slowed down instead of picking up. She sternly told me, "I am going to leave you; you need to stop thinking and get into your Zen. I will then come back at lunch time to check on you." *Lunch time?!* I was shocked. I arrived at 6:30 a.m. She basically scared the Zen into me. No more phone, no more planning. I surrendered to my body. Back contractions at 3 cm felt like a never-ending painful tease, so when my midwife returned to my relaxed state of 3 cm, I almost flipped out. Thankfully, she had an option. If I gave her the green light, she would break my water. I had received all the antibiotics for Baby and me, but the disclaimer was I risked getting a storm of contractions— back contractions. I often share the wise American advice, "Go big or go home!" In this case, I didn't want to go home without my baby in my arms! I decided to sail into the eye of this storm!

She broke my water at 1:00 p.m., at 3 cm dilated. She told me she would not go far because in an hour or so, I would start feeling more intensity. I laid back into my fetal position, took the last glance I can remember of my wave poster, laid there naked and with my eyes closed, breathing in the lovely smell of lavender and humming to the relaxing music I had playing in the background. I went into a deep state of meditation that I was very proud of. The wave I imagined coming over me was okay, and in between waves, I could tread water…until I felt a tidal wave was approaching. Holy sh*t, I am going to drown! I yelled, "Get-t-t he-e-er! She better be close!"

BECAUSE YOU ARE SUPERWOMAN

Only about five minutes passed since the warm water I felt between my legs turned into a major tidal wave of contractions. My husband was apprehensive at first to call the midwife back prematurely (again), but when my voice dropped three octaves and was on the verge of sounding demonic, he got that woman fast!

Ten minutes later, and the equivalent of three tsunami waves, the midwife arrived. She looked at me and asked, "So, what do you think of me now?"

This was not a time for sarcasm. I opened my eyes abruptly, glared and said, "I do not like you. How could you do this to me?!"

No one has ever looked so pleased with these words before. She responded, "Well, that was quicker than expected, but baby is definitely making his or her way now." She insisted I try out a hot shower as this can be helpful for back labor. Butt naked, I stumbled to the bathroom between contractions, sat down, and let the warm water flow against my back. I ordered a change of music because at some point, some Dutch folk music made its way into my Chillax playlist. About an hour passed before my cheery midwife approached me and wanted to check my progress. That meant I needed to move out of the shower. Naked and wet, I made it back to the bed. It was well worth it when I heard, "Wow, seven centimeters!" From three to seven in under an hour. She assured me she would no longer leave the room. She also put pressure on my back during contractions.

At this point, I was on all fours. And then I started to feel my body have urges to push. I grunted, "MUSIC, Change…the… playlist. Push playlist." My husband was on it, and I felt a slight smirk come over me when I heard Snoop Dog tell me to "Sweat." Another nurse had made her way into the room, and I remember her smiling, "Het is gezellig hier!" which translates to, "It's fun and cozy in here!"

Sia was singing "Alive" in the background. I am not sure how my midwife knew it, but she insisted I change positions. My contractions were slowing down; not what we wanted! But, I didn't feel like I had enough time, nor energy, between contractions to move.

Through tough, direct "Dutch love," I was convinced to move. I wanted to stand with the help of the bed. As soon as I was standing, the urge to push became much more intense. I could tell my body was in a primal place by the type of low moans escaping from my throat. I remember pain—but trumping that pain was power, happiness and laughter. I remember opening my eyes and looking at my midwife and saying, "Is it too late for an epidural?" I knew the answer, but it was my turn to be funny. She laughed.

To the beat of the music, I was pushing, dancing, and grunting the baby down! I was at 9 cm. At some point during your labor marathon, you are just exhausted. I needed to change positions again. The transitions were the worst at the time, but hindsight tells me they were the key!

What should my next position be? We went through the list. Labor ball, no. In the bed laying on my back, hell no. Bed laying on my side, no. At this point in labor, I felt like a superhero. It seemed that a proper superhero must be on her feet! *But* my legs were Jell-O. So, when she offered the oldest and most common Dutch labor position, I agreed. "Baarkruk (translation: Bar stool), YES!"

I sat on the stool with my husband behind me, and the midwife crouched down on the ground under me. Immediately, when I sat, I felt an entire new world of pain crash down on me. Even superheroes have moments of mental weakness, and this was mine. The head was crowning, and I couldn't get the song "Ring of Fire" by Johnny Cash out of my head. I grunted and pleaded, "Please tell me the shoulders don't hurt as much as the head!"

I just couldn't go through that pain again (shout out to all the mamas of multiples, you are superheroes on a whole other level!) My midwife held out a mirror, "Do you want to see?"

I don't like scary movies, and in the moment, this felt like one, so my answer was, "NO!"

I never did get an answer to my question about the shoulders. But after two pushes, the head was out! After that it felt like the rest of my baby just slid out! I still don't know if this is normal, and my baby did not have an abnormally large head, but after the head, the body just felt like a slither and a tickle.

Immediately, my baby was placed on my chest. I was elated with joy and love. At some point while I was in the clouds with my baby, the nurse asked what the name was. My husband and I were like, well is it a boy or girl? We wanted it to be a surprise. I gently detached this little human from my chest to check out the private parts. Before I could process any further, we, including both our neighbors in the rooms next to us, and maybe the entire maternity ward heard, "Piemel! It's a piemel!" This means penis in Dutch. My husband was overjoyed.

His name is Leonardo Joseph Willem Drent. He was born with his American roots intact; he came out to the song "Hey Ya" by Outkast. It was three hours after my water broke and just twenty minutes of pushing. The entire birth marathon began with a slow warm-up, but it ended with a blazing sprint!

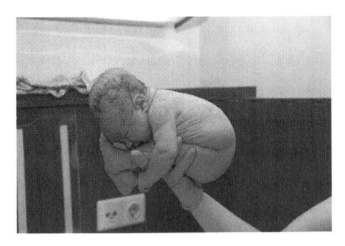
His positioning in the womb

The rest is history. He was, and is, perfect. And that is why through the difficulties, scary moments, pain, and all that is usually associated with giving birth, for me it was the most empowering, exciting, and above all, joyous occasion in my life. I want to remember every part of this miraculous event. My son is eight months old as I write this story; I am still in awe of the incredible joy I am filled with every time I think back on that day.

Just three hours after giving birth, we were able to bring our son home. I said goodbye to the awesome staff, one nurse and one midwife. There was no reason we had to stay because our care would continue at home. That very evening, our "at home nurse" came by. She was with us for six to eight hours a day, for the next eight days. The Dutch include this ongoing maternity care as part of their universal healthcare policy. Try Googling Kraamzorg to find out more. The nurse showed us how to wash the baby, offered tips and tricks for newborn care, examined me and how I was healing, offered breast-feeding support, and performed light chores around the house. This type of care was monumental in supporting the physical and emotional transition into parenthood. Care in the Netherlands does not just focus on the new baby; it recognizes how the health of the family ultimately plays into the health of the baby. Every time I closed my eyes for a post-partum nap while the nurse cared for my baby, I thanked the Dutch for truly understanding a woman's needs.

13 HEATHER'S BIRTH STORY: FROM THE BOARD ROOM TO THE DELIVERY ROOM

MEET HEATHER –

1. Education: associate's degree from Saddleback College, CA

2. Primary Job During Pregnancy: Vice President/Residential Lender of a mortgage company

3. Age at Delivery: 33

4. Two Ways I Prepared My Mind for Birth: By attending Lamaze classes and focusing on breathing

5. Ways I Prepared My Body for Birth: Keeping active, relaxing in the sunshine in a bikini, eating healthy (except for those Macho Egg Burrito cravings from El Conejo!)

6. Birth Location: San Clemente, CA - San Clemente General Hospital

7. Delivery Date: Two weeks early!

8. Present at Birth: Husband, OB-GYN, nurse

9. Did I Prefer Contractions or Pushing? Pushing felt better to me.

10. Two Resources I Recommend to Others Preparing for Birth: Taking the Lamaze class made me more aware of my body and what to expect. Keeping a positive attitude and working up to the day I had my baby worked best for me.

11. Have I, or Would I, Aim for Another Minimal Intervention Birth after Experiencing It? I planned to with my second child. He ended up being a planned c-section because he was breached *and* sunny side up!

I was the owner of a mortgage lending corporation, and it was a very busy time in the industry. I worked up until the day my first child was born. In fact, the day I went into labor, I was to lead a power point presentation to clients. I had stayed up preparing the night before.

I woke up at 6:00 a.m. on the day of the presentation, went to the bathroom, and my water broke while sitting on the toilet! I felt lucky that it happened that way. I was completely effaced for a week and 4 cm dilated, so contractions began immediately once my water broke. I called work to let them know I was in labor and would not be able to attend the meeting.

I was planning on a natural birth, and my husband and I were in the process of attending Lamaze classes, so I wanted to wait things out at home. I was positive that I wanted to shower and shave my legs before leaving for the hospital. While I did this, the contractions were getting closer and closer together. My husband was monitoring me and getting very anxious about leaving.

We left for San Clemente, from Orange, a thirty-two-mile drive during rush hour. It took us one hour to get to San Clemente General. During the ride, my feet started on the floor but moved to the windshield as I was sure the baby was going to be delivered in a Jeep Cherokee.

We arrived at the hospital at 8:00 a.m., checked in, and I was 8 cm dilated. The hospital quickly created wristbands for me and the baby. From there, it felt like someone hit the fast forward button. The feelings were intense. I felt like I would be sick; I could feel my baby moving downward.

At 8:37 a.m., I was holding my precious, little redhead. I felt an immediate connection to her because her hair was the same color as my father's. It was wonderful to not use any drugs, as after the baby arrived, I felt great and was free to move around!

In fact, I asked if I could go home a few hours later. The hospital told me I could not, as I had a slight fever. It turned out to work in our favor; the hospital had a beautiful dinner for my husband and I, and I had some exclusive time with my baby girl.

My friend who does income taxes had a baby shower for me.

Since my baby arrived two weeks early, I took my little girl to the baby shower, two days after giving birth! It was a fun twist on a baby shower. It was exciting to open presents with friends *and* let them see the baby.

Two months later, I went back to work. I was the bread winner at the time, and I felt it was important to take care of my family financially. I enjoyed being in the office by day and snuggling my new baby each night when I came home.

14 TINA'S BIRTH STORY: BEING YOUR OWN BIRTH ADVOCATE IS CHALLENGING, BUT HIGHLY WORTH IT!

MEET TINA –

1. Education: California State University San Bernardino, bachelor's in Business Administration//Walden University, master's in Industrial & Organizational Psychology

2. Primary Job During Pregnancy: Sr. Organizational Development Consultant

3. Age at Delivery: 32

4. Two Ways I Prepared My Mind for Birth: I read the *Mama Natural Week-by-Week Guide to Pregnancy and Childbirth* by Genevieve Howland and *Mindful Birthing* by Nancy Bardacke. I also took the Hypnobabies class with my husband (six-week course).

5. Two Ways I Prepared My Body for Birth: I took daily

BECAUSE YOU ARE SUPERWOMAN

supplements to support myself and the baby. Those supplements included: whole food based prenatals by Garden of Life, Cod Liver Oil (for DHA and Omega), Turmeric (for my joint pain and to reduce inflammation), Garlic pill (to keep me healthy), and I ate mainly organic. I also made sure to exercise every day, even if it was just walking.

6. City/State of Birth: Irvine, CA

7. Location of Birth: Kaiser Hospital in Irvine, CA

8. Delivery Date: I delivered on my due date, August 18, at 40 weeks.

9. Present at Birth: My husband, my doula (who was also my best friend), and a midwife who delivered my son

10. Did I Prefer Contractions or Pushing? This is a hard question because both were so different. My contractions lasted for about thirty hours and pushing only lasted around thirty minutes. I would say the contractions because I got into a routine of how to manage them with hypnosis.

11. Two Resources I Recommend to Others Preparing for Birth: Hypnobabies class for education about what to expect from your body, the hospital, natural options, etc. This class covers everything from nutrition to what to expect. Learning how to manage your pain is an incredible tool. Also, I would recommend the book: *Mama Natural Week-by-Week Guide to Pregnancy and Childbirth* by Genevieve Howland. It is absolutely incredible and resourceful.

189

12. Have I, or Would I, Aim for Another Minimal Intervention Birth After Experiencing It? Yes, I would. It is totally doable.

13. My Empowering Message to Women Considering a Minimal Intervention Birth Plan: The key is to understand, when you're in the moment, that it WON'T last forever and the discomfort is just temporary. Nothing in life worth anything significant comes easily and no exception is made with birthing your child. Having a positive mindset is key. Realizing and embracing that you and your baby are going on this journey together, partnering together, to bring him/her into the world, is truly something to smile about and embrace.

Like many women, my first trimester was awful. My husband and I had been married for six months and knew early on we were ready to try for a family. So, we quickly started down that path. I actually found out I was pregnant while on a business trip to Dubai; I was representing a major player in the avionics industry. On my flight back to California, I caught a cold on the plane, which morphed into a nasty cough. Every time I coughed, it triggered my gag reflex, and I would throw up, which made going to work super unpleasant. This finally cleared up by the second trimester, and my body did a complete 360. The second trimester, I felt AMAZING. I was super active, eating healthy, and my energy level was at a ten. My third trimester was very similar. In fact, I continued to feel great up until the day I delivered!

The idea of a natural birth was something that started to interest me about five years before even getting pregnant. After going on a journey of changing my diet, studying traditional Chinese medicine and essential oils, and learning to be preventative with my body, I liked the idea of allowing my body to do what it was made to do when it came to giving birth. I was 100% open to medical intervention if I, or my baby, were in an emergency situation and our health was poor, but otherwise, I wanted to let my body work its magic. When I told family and friends about my birth plan, I think half were supportive, but half clearly were not. I was repeatedly told, "Everyone wants to do it naturally, but when you are in the moment, everything changes." Some people even told me, "Don't try and be a hero. Just do what the doctors tell you; they know more than you."

But because I had already learned how powerful and miraculous the human body really is, it was life changing. My body was made to birth life, and I wanted to experience what that felt like, whether it was good or bad. I was made for this. This was my experience to partner with my baby and be a part of

BECAUSE YOU ARE SUPERWOMAN

his entrance into the world. I wanted to remember that drug free. I knew I was firm in my choices, but I didn't realize how much push back I would continue to encounter right up until the birth of my son!

The day before my due date, I called Briana, my friend and doula, and told her I felt as if the time was getting close for my son, Aksel, to be born. She said she wanted to drive down and spend the weekend with me and my husband Bjorn. She arrived around 8:00 p.m. We all sat up and chatted, had some food, and she used a pregnancy tuning fork on my belly. It sent vibrations through my belly, and Aksel responded with movements and kicking. It was a special bonding moment for us all. We stayed up late and into the early hours of the next day. Briana and Bjorn went to sleep around 1:00 a.m., and I laid awake in bed because at forty weeks pregnant, I was starting to have a hard time sleeping. Before getting into bed, I put some drops of Clary Sage essential oil, diluted with fractionated coconut oil on my ankles and wrists (note: Clary Sage should only be used toward the end of pregnancy. It helps relieve pain, promotes/induces labor, and eases childbirth). I then got into bed and was on my phone, scrolling Amazon, looking at post-partum pregnancy wraps that I wanted to buy for after the baby was born. It was 3:15 a.m. and I felt a pop down below in my vagina. It sounded like a rubber band snapping. I wasn't sure what the noise was but knew I wanted to get up and go to the bathroom to check it out. As soon as I got up I felt water rushing out and that is when I knew my water had broken. In the bathroom there was m o r e water and a "bloody show" to confirm that yes, Aksel was going to make his appearance soon!

I woke Bjorn up, and he went and woke Briana up. I started having some contractions right away. We wanted to measure how far apart the contractions were for the next hour, so I decided to flat iron my hair while we waited (every woman has her priorities). The contractions were about three minutes apart and lasted for about 30–60 seconds at a time. They felt like intense period cramps. We decided to head to Kaiser Hospital and check in. I thought for sure Aksel would be coming soon because of how quickly the contractions started and how close they were together for the past hour.

We arrived at Kaiser at about 5:45 a.m. on my due date. I called ahead to Labor & Delivery and told them that we were on our way there, and they said they would have a room ready for me. I learned in the Hypnobabies class that if your water breaks, you can take a pad soaked with the amniotic fluid, and they can test it with a PH paper to ensure that your water has actually broken. I brought the pad for them to test so I could bypass the vaginal check. I wanted as little vaginal intervention as possible. Sure enough, they tested my pad, confirmed my water had broken, and admitted me into the hospital without a vaginal check! Right away, a nurse came in and started collecting information and asked for our birth plan. Briana and Bjorn started setting up the room with Hypnobabies affirmations that we printed off and Briana set up some essential oils for me on the table next to me. She had essential oils and a Himalayan salt sniffer for me to inhale while controlling my breathing.

The on-call OB walked in and said that she would brief me and go over my birth plan, in lieu of the midwife. At my hospital, all healthy mothers were assigned a midwife, and women with complicated pregnancies were assigned OBs. Up until that point, all of my prenatal care had been with a midwife. I was visibly frustrated because I had specifically requested having a midwife, and not an OB. The OB said that she could honor the majority of the birth plan but had a big problem with me declining an IV or a hep-lock. She proceeded to tell me how she had watched multiple women die of hemorrhages and wanted to make sure it didn't happen to me. She also said she recommended Pitocin, and they could only administer it through an IV. I told her I did not want any medical intervention, as long as myself and the baby were healthy, and would be doing the birth drug and intervention-free. She then proceeded to tell me what "she would do" and really pushed me and made me uncomfortable. My contractions, up until that OB came in, were close together, about three minutes apart, but started to slow down when I began to feel uncomfortable (not feeling safe to birth) and had to question my birth choices all over again. My contractions slowed down from being three minutes apart to about 10–15 minutes apart.

I am a firm believer, and also learned in the Hypnobabies class, that when we don't feel safe and secure, we hold our baby in and don't feel comfortable proceeding with birth until we feel safe and secure. This woman DID NOT make me feel safe and secure. She was using scare tactics to get me to do what was comfortable for her. I politely declined again, and I was asked to sign a waiver, which I did. Thankfully, this OB's shift was over, and she was leaving.

My mom came around 7:00 a.m., and we had a short visit because she had to go to work. I wanted to keep the visitors in my room to a minimum, and wanted few distractions and a positive environment since I was using Hypnobabies tracks and not having any drugs or intervention. The shift changed and a midwife named Paige came in and introduced herself to me. She said she was fine with my birth plan but wanted to do a cervical check to see how far dilated I was. I told her I did not want any cervical checks and wanted baby Aksel to come when he was ready, and I would be listening to my body for cues. I believed my body was made to do this, and I was confident I would know when it would be time to push and time to welcome our little boy into the world. This midwife did not like my answer and wanted to check me anyway. She told me she understood I wanted to be birthing naturally, but she really thought I should get checked. I declined. The only thing they came in consistently to do was take my temperature. Since my water broke and I declined the GBS testing, they intermittently hooked me to a fetal heart rate monitor to check Aksel's heart rate and make sure it wasn't dropping. I enjoyed that I did not have anything hooked to me and did not have to ingest any medication. I was having contractions and listening to my Hypnobabies tracks and breathing through them. Briana went on a Starbucks run for me and got me an iced green tea latte with coconut milk. I was also eating some snacks like antibiotic-free, free-range beef jerky, smoothie fruit packs, and some Young Living Ningxia red packs. I was also drinking a lot of coconut water and Essentia to stay hydrated.

By about noon, my sister stopped by with some lunch for me, Bjorn, and Briana. At that point, I was starving, and I gobbled up a chicken sandwich and a lemonade. It was delicious, and it gave me energy to keep going. I started getting more intense contractions, and they were about three minutes apart again. I was getting to a point where I was unable to sit or lay down; I was only able to walk, lean, or be on all fours on the bed. Every time I contracted, I was leaking amniotic fluid and blood. I kept getting pressured by the midwife to get checked to see how far along I was. I kept politely rejecting the request. I wanted my baby boy to come when he was ready and stay positive the entire time. I knew if they checked me, it would deter me from staying positive because if I thought I was ready to have him, but they said I was only 3 cm dilated, it could be very discouraging. I wanted as little cervical inter-vention as possible because my water broke, and I wanted to ensure I didn't expose myself to any unnecessary infections. I also only accepted the fetal monitoring every few hours as it was getting exhausting and very distracting for the nurse to come in and break me out of my hypnosis.

I kept getting a lot of pressure from the midwife to get checked. My actual midwife was not on staff that day, and the midwife on the mid-day shift seemed annoyed with me. She again told me she "gets the whole wanting to birth naturally thing" but really suggested that I get checked. I asked her what purpose it would serve, and she said it would be knowledge for us all. I told her I was confident my body would let me know when the time was ready, and she started laughing and walked out of the room.

My actual midwife ended up calling me around 4:30 p.m. and asked how I was doing, and I told her what was going on. She said she thought at that point it would be a good idea to get checked at least once because I was doing hypnosis for pain management and I should know which track to play, the birthing waves track or the pushing track. She said her only concern was that I would start pushing before it was time and rip my cervix.

I relented and finally allowed the midwife on staff to check me, and it was the most painful experience ever. I yelped out in pain, but she didn't stop. I told her she needed to stop at that very moment. She said I was only dilated 5 cm and wasn't ready for pushing. That was exactly why I didn't want to know. It felt so discouraging to hear baby wasn't ready at that moment. I know myself, and I needed all the positivity I could get to work together with my baby boy and support him in his homecoming. I asked when that midwife was going home, and I was told she was off at 6:30 p.m. I told myself, and

Aksel, that we would wait until after she was off because I did not want her delivering my precious boy. I didn't want anyone telling me when Aksel would be born, only God knew when his birth would be. Aksel would let my body know when he was ready for us to get him out. At the end of the day, we are mammals, and we will only release and allow for birth when our body feels safe and secure.

I was feeling a bit exhausted and frustrated at that point because I still couldn't sit or lay down; I could only lean and that was exhausting. I was still contracting every couple of minutes, and it was starting to feel like the movie Groundhog Day where the same thing just kept happening over and over. Briana was giving me many lower back massages, using her tuning fork, a sound bowl on my lower back, essential oils, and keeping me calm. A sound bowl is used to reduce stress, anxiety, improve circulation, increase blood flow, provide deep relaxation, balance your chakras, increase mental and emotional clarity, and promote well-being. It is traditionally used in meditation. I found it very relaxing, and the sound frequencies were helpful during contracting. My husband, Bjorn, was rocking with me through all my contractions while I was standing and kept positive, giving me loving affir-mations.

Then a medical godsend entered my room.

Her name was Sarah. She was a nurse who came on duty and was the most encouraging, affirming, and sweet soul I had ever met. She affirmed me for my courage to birth the way I was, and when I would contract, she would come put my arms around her neck and we would rock together. She reminded me that I could do this, and I was doing great. She gave me that mental push I needed. Also, a new midwife came on duty, and she was the nicest midwife thus far. I was beyond ecstatic. I let Aksel know he was safe to come out whenever he was ready, and I was ready to work together with him to meet him.

From 7:00 p.m. until about 10:45 p.m. I spent my time in the bathroom squatting, leaning, and rocking through the contractions. I was so exhausted from standing that I went to the bed and got help to lay on my side for just a few minutes. Within thirty minutes, my body just started pushing. It was an incredible, primal feeling. I was not in control of the pushing; my body was just doing it. I made very deep moans and screams while pushing. It was nothing I could control; it just came out. I did not feel like I was in a lot of pain. All I felt was a bit of a burning feeling in my vagina. We called the midwife in, and she walked in calm and unaffected. She thought I was pushing when I wasn't ready. She said, "You were only 5 cm; there is no way you are ready to push in only a few hours."

I couldn't speak during the contractions and pushing, but during the brief breaks I got, I turned to her and said I wasn't controlling it and that my body was just doing it. She said she would check. She lifted up my leg and checked and said, "Yup, he's on his way out. You're having a baby!"

I knew my body would let me know when Aksel was ready.

This is what we were made to do! I kept pushing, and they asked if I wanted a mirror to see what was happening. I accepted because I couldn't wait to see my little man. Instead of coming out skull first, he came out face first, so I just saw a face coming out of my vagina. It was very alien looking. I thought I would just see a crown of a head, but I saw eyes, a nose, and a mouth instead. Then I stopped looking but kept pushing.

The midwife and nurses were very encouraging and everything was going great until they got quiet and started whispering among each other. My husband Bjorn was at the head of the bed with me holding my hand, and Briana was in the action zone with the midwifes and nurses. A nurse asked me if I could change positions. Now I started getting annoyed. I just wanted to meet my little boy and be done with the pushing, and they were now asking me to change positions in the middle of pushing? I said, "No, this is fine."

They encouraged me to try another position. I repeated, "NO!"

In a serious tone, she said, "Tina, he is stuck. His shoulder is stuck, and we need to move you to get him out, otherwise he could get paralyzed."

I quickly agreed. I think they didn't want to scare me initially, but I wouldn't budge, so they told me the truth. They all helped me, and I flipped on all fours on the bed. A few minutes later, my beautiful, precious, little Aksel boy was born at 11:21 p.m. on his due date, weighing in at 9 lbs., 4 oz. Aksel and I did it! He came out perfect and healthy, regardless of his shoulder getting stuck.

They got me on my back. I had provided my own soft muslin blanket for them to put him in and asked them not to wipe off the vernix. Of course, they started wiping it, and I asked them to stop. They put him in my arms, and Bjorn and I looked down at our precious little bundle in wonder.

Then came the fun part of trying to latch him to breastfeed, trying to clean me up, and also bringing in a "specialist" to stitch me up because I tore from front to back. There were so many things happening all at once, and I was so exhausted. I asked them if I could just have a few minutes to bond with my baby and my husband without being poked and prodded.

BECAUSE YOU ARE SUPERWOMAN

They said no, they didn't want me to hemorrhage. I completely understood but man, this new mama just needed a minute to breathe! Once it was all said and done, I made them do all the tests on Aksel while he was on me, and they weighed him next to me. I opted in for the Vitamin K shot for him, because it is supposed to help stop the bleeding from circumcision. I delayed the antibiotic eye drops until the next day to let his body's gut flora build up. I had a great nurse the next day who only put a dab of the eye drops in his eyes and didn't even use 80% of the antibiotic eyedrops pouch. I declined the Hep B vaccine for him, as I felt he did not need a vaccine in his delicate immune system the day he entered the world. They also took a blood test to make sure Aksel didn't have GBS (since I declined testing for it), and it came out negative so he didn't need any additional treatment. They escorted our new family to our own room, where Bjorn told me to nap and rest, and he would stay up with Aksel (Husband of the Year).

I was exhausted and a bit sore down there, but otherwise, I felt like myself, alert and very accomplished. I made sure I had my essential oil blends, my food-based prenatal, coconut water, and Ningxia Red to drink to give myself natural energy. I fought many people and signed many waivers to have my baby boy the way I wanted to, but I did it, with God's grace, of course.

15 ANNA'S BIRTH STORY: HAVING AN "ADVANCED MATERNAL AGE" DOESN'T MAKE YOUR BODY INCAPABLE

MEET ANNA –

1. Education: Northwood University – Hotel Restaurant Resort Management

2. Primary Job During Pregnancy: Mill Operator

3. Age at Delivery: 35

4. Two Ways I Prepared My Mind for Birth: Read Ina May's book and studied pain coping techniques

5. Two Ways I Prepared My Body for Birth: Lots of squats, rolling on yoga ball

6. City/State of Birth: Colorado Springs, CO

7. Location of Birth: Hospital

8. Delivery Date: 39 weeks + 3 days

9. Present at Birth: midwife, nurses, husband

10. Did I Prefer Contractions or Pushing? Contractions

11. One Resource I Recommend to Others Preparing for Birth: Ina May's book

12. Have I, or Would I, Aim for Another Minimal Intervention Birth After Experiencing It? Yes.

13. My Empowering Message to Women Considering a Minimal Intervention Birth Plan: Don't be afraid of the pain. It has a purpose!

When I first found out I was pregnant, I was scared, anxious, and happy. I was going to be bringing another life into this world. As the months progressed and the more research I did, I knew I wanted to try to bring this little human into the world as naturally as possible. After reading stories of epidurals not working or only working on one side and being stuck in a bed because your legs are numb, in addition to the side effects it could have on my child (making baby drowsy, slowing down baby's heart rate, slowing down labor), going without any pain medication sounded like the best option t o me.

One thing that kept me in this mindset was that thousands of women, over thousands of years, delivered their babies without medicine, and they survived and thrived after their birth. Knowing that modern medicine has made it very safe to have babies compared to one hundred years ago, I felt very comfortable going the "au natural" route.

My midwife's office was very receptive to me giving birth with minimal intervention, and the hospital I was going to be delivering at was well equipped for natural births. They had showers and tubs to help you relax. I was allowed to bring my diffuser in, and they had birthing bars on all their beds and exercise balls for you to utilize during your labor. I had my diffuser going, but I didn't notice it after a while. So I'm not sure if it helped me in labor or not.

Due to my advanced maternal age of thirty-five, I was informed that I would not be allowed to go past forty weeks gestation. I had been scheduled for induction at thirty-nine weeks and five days. At my thirty-nine-week appointment I

BECAUSE YOU ARE SUPERWOMAN

had my membranes swept to see if I could go into labor naturally.

That night, at 1:00 a.m., I awoke to the sensation of needing to go to the bathroom—not unusual at this stage in the game. On my short walk to the bathroom, I started to feel water dripping down my leg, so I started to run. I barely made it to the toilet when I had a big gush of water come out. I was pretty sure my water had broken. It took a good couple minutes for the water to stop. When it did, I waddled back to my bedroom to get my cellphone to call my parents. I was home alone, since my husband was working out of town. Thankfully, my parents had come to town and were staying in a nearby hotel in anticipation of my baby's birth.

Once my parents arrived, we decided to go to the hospital, since it was an hour and a half away. I called my husband to let him know what was going on and got dressed, and we drove to the hospital. At that time, I was still not having any contractions, so I was very nervous about how long it would be before my contractions would start, and if they would start all on their own.

By the time we made it to the hospital at 2:30 a.m., my contractions had started, but they were very mild and about five minutes apart. The nurses in triage hooked me up to the monitor and had me get in a gown. I was dilated to 3 cm. My contractions were starting to get stronger, and I started throwing up because of the pain. They moved me into a room and had me get comfortable.

I knew from research I could sit on an exercise ball to help relax my hips. So, I sat on the ball, moving in circles as my contractions grew stronger.

After another two hours, I felt the need to go to the bathroom (#2). When I had arrived, the nurses warned me that if I felt the sensation to go #2, I needed to let them know. Apparently, they had an incident where a woman felt she needed to go #2 and instead pushed her baby out while sitting on the toilet. They did not want that happening to me, so I was told to carefully try to go but not to push too hard. After that, the midwife checked me again, and I was dilated to 9 cm.

I did my research on pain management techniques. However, in the end, no one talks about dealing with the pain while pushing; all the advice was about making it to transition, and they left it at that. It made it sound like the contractions before, and during, transition were the hardest part. In my experience, pushing ended up being the hardest part.

Thankfully, my husband finally made it to the hospital just in time, because I felt the need to push. The midwife told me I had to wait until I was fully dilated. After three more contractions, in which I had to try not to push, even though I had the urge, I was told I could start pushing.

I had chosen to lay on my side while pushing, as this seemed the most comfortable. However, as I started to push, my pain all started to come from my back. At the time, I had no idea what it meant, so I tried to focus on pushing and not the pain.

The midwife had me switch sides from where I was laying as I continued to push. After a little while, I had to switch sides again. This continued for close to an hour. I knew deep down they were having me switch sides because baby's heart rate was starting to drop, and it would come back up as soon as I would switch sides.

At the end of an hour of pushing, my midwife finally told me I had to push the baby out now! The sudden outburst of tough love scared me into action. I had to push with all my might.

It was shift change for the nurses, and there was a new group of nurses that came in to help me. One nurse in particular came up with the idea to tie two knots in a sheet and give me one knot while she held the other knot. This allowed me to get up on top of my stomach and push more on the baby than pushing with my back.

At this point I was so exhausted, I didn't want to do it anymore. I could feel the baby entering the birth canal, and it was painful. I did not want to push any harder.

Since I knew that the baby's heart rate was starting to show signs of distress, I knew I had to push past all the pain and get him out ASAP. So, while holding onto the sheet, I finally found the strength to push past the pain and push him all the way out.

At 7:21 a.m., my sweet little one came out facing up! That is why I had such bad back pain! He came out screaming and alert. I had done it! Immediately, he was given to me. While they cleaned him up a little bit, we cuddled, and I could finally relax…until I needed to deliver the placenta.

Apparently, people that live at higher elevations have bigger placenta's than people at sea level. They gave me Pitocin to help get the placenta out and some IV pain meds to help dull the pain. I accepted it because I no longer had to worry that a high dose of medication was entering my baby's tiny body since he was now earth-side. The placenta finally came out, and the midwife stitched me up.

In a little over six hours, from start to finish, I had my little baby boy in my arms!

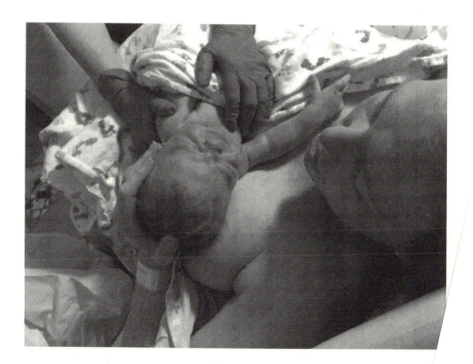

16 TAHLIA'S BIRTH STORIES: GIVE ME MORE (BABIES, NOT DRUGS)!

MEET TAHLIA –

1. Education: Santa Monica College with associate's in Accounting

2. Primary Job During Pregnancy: Chocolatier, Gourmet Chocolate Shop

3. Age at Delivery: Baby One: 26, Baby Two: 31

4. Two Ways I Prepared My Mind for Birth: Think positive (the second time, I remembered how strong I was the first time I gave birth) and visualize the moment when you get to hold your newborn.

5. Two Ways I Prepared My Body for Birth: Kegels/exercise and eating healthy

6. City/State of Birth: Laguna Hills, CA (both babies)

7. Location of Birth: Saddleback Women's Hospital (both babies)

8. Delivery Date: Baby One: Exactly 40 weeks, Baby Two: 40 weeks + 1 Day

9. Present at Birth: Baby One: My husband, Brennan, four nurses, and OB-GYN doctor; Baby Two: My husband, three nurses, and OB-GYN doctor

10. Did I Prefer Contractions or Pushing? Baby One: Pushing was better! Baby Two: Contractions were strong, but I could distract myself by talking/breathing during them.

11. Two Resources I Recommend to Others Preparing for Birth: Baby One: I would consider researching online and watching home videos of natural birth, and to have a mind set on giving yourself the power and will to go all natural. Baby Two: During this pregnancy, I didn't do much research since I remembered quite a bit from my first pregnancy. Although I did research on the internet if there were some things I had forgotten about. One website I do recommend is Baby Center, and there is an app for that as well.

12. Have I, or Would I, Aim for Another Minimal Intervention Birth After Experiencing It? Baby One: Yes, I would definitely do another natural birth after experiencing this one. Baby Two: This was more painful than my first natural birth, and I would still do it again, no matter what!

13. My Empowering Message to Women Considering a Minimal Intervention Birth Plan: Any woman can give birth naturally by giving themselves the right mindset of strength to handle the pain. The contractions can be exhausting over time while in labor, but tell yourself you can get through it and distract yourself with happy thoughts of the future you're about to have with your newborn.

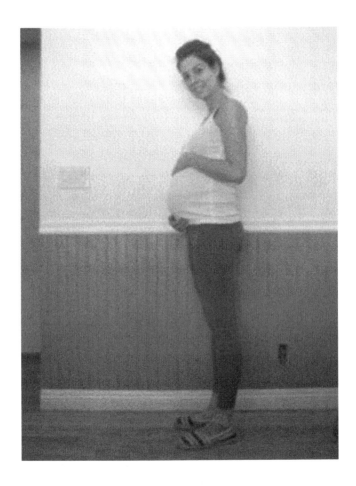

Baby One

I come from a strong lineage of women who were confident in their natural ability to give birth.

My own mother, and various other women in our family, inspired me to want and prepare for a minimal intervention, natural birth. It was in my genes. It just felt right to me to experience how amazing our bodies can be and feel in control of birth. I didn't want any interventions slowing my labor or harming my baby. My husband was very supportive of my decision.

But with pregnancy and childbirth, surprises are a bit inevitable. For two months during the last trimester, my baby was breech. Just a few weeks before my due date, my doctor told me that I would have to have a c-section if she didn't turn. I tried all the techniques to get my baby to turn like "follow the light," squatting, and walking. I'm not sure what worked, but she did eventually get her act together and turn head down.

It all started on June 21, after I went in for my last checkup with my doctor. He did a cervical check and said I was 2–3 cm dilated and 20% effaced. After he finished, he told me I had a "bloody show." I didn't realize that this would be the start of a long, slow labor.

By that time, it was 10:00 a.m. I went home that day, feeling great and "normal," so I went on about my daily routine. My mom stopped by to check up on me and declared, "You'll have two more weeks."

Her assumption was based on the fact that she went two weeks late with me. I heard her words, but in my heart, I was hoping for my baby girl to be born on the twenty-second.

It wasn't until 2:00 p.m. that I started feeling light cramps. I wasn't startled or worried, but I remember being unsure if it was a contraction or not. So, I let it be and continued about my day. I took a nice long shower, painted my nails, and relaxed. By 5:00 p.m., I noticed these "cramps/contractions" were coming quite frequently, so I started timing them myself. Every 20–30 minutes, I had a contraction lasting about thirty seconds. This went on for five hours!

From 10:00 p.m.–2:00 a.m. the frequency went to every 15–20 minutes apart, lasting for 30–45 seconds. I remember feeling uneasy. I constantly had the urge to go to the bathroom. I couldn't sit still or lay down and sleep.

After 2:00 a.m., things got super intense. I was constantly moving around to distract myself from the pain I was having each time a contraction rolled around. I vacuumed my whole house, walked around in circles (outside at 3:00 a.m.), sat and bounced on my exercise ball, and took three short showers *and* a bath.

I knew I had a pretty high pain tolerance from when I got a tattoo on my foot and I was able to mentally distract myself from the pain, so I wasn't screaming my head off, but, whoa!

My husband couldn't tell what to make of me; he actually thought I wasn't in labor and went to bed! I actually didn't mind it, though, because there was nothing for him to do. I told him I'd let him know if it was "time." I just kept tracking my time of the contractions all the way until 4:00 a.m., which by then were five minutes apart and one minute long. I started questioning myself if this was the "time" to go to the hospital or not, because I did not want to have to be put into the evaluation room and wonder if they'd send me home, telling me I wasn't ready. I took the chance, woke my husband up, and said, "Let's go!"

He looked at me and was like, "You're not in labor; there's no way! You're not screaming!"

Ha, I thought. But a tiny piece of me was nervous he was right. We left the house a little after 5:00 a.m. Since it was early, my husband wanted to grab Starbucks before heading to the hospital. I thanked my guardian angel when they were closed! We drove straight to the hospital and walked in to the emergency room, leaving all our stuff in the car, to sign in. While we waited for the nurse to come grab me, another couple rushed in and the husband was frantically asking for a wheelchair for his laboring wife. When they offered me a wheelchair, I refused. I wanted to walk to distract myself from the pain. Since looks can be deceiving, they put me in an evaluation room, and whisked the other woman into the delivery room.

It was around 5:20 a.m. They had me undress, put on a gown,

BECAUSE YOU ARE SUPERWOMAN

and pee in a cup. They put me on the bed and strapped me to the fetal monitor. The minute I laid down, I said I needed to throw up. The nurse quickly got me a bag and up came the Snickers bar I had earlier that morning between my contractions. At the time, it had tasted so good, but the second time I tasted it, it was not so good. After yacking, I looked at my husband and gestured, "Something happened *down there*."

The nurse looked under the sheet and told us that my water broke. She never did give me an update on how dilated I was. Instead, everyone started to rush around like something was on fire! I was pretty calm the whole time because I didn't even know what to do with myself. While wheeling me toward my delivery room, the nurse turned to my husband and asked if he was ready with the camera. Of course, we had left everything in the car, so he rushed out to grab it.

The minute I was put into my room, I had that urge to push. I told the nurses this, and they were running around frantically, prepping everything. One nurse was trying to put an IV in my arm. She was obviously nervous and couldn't find my vein (four times). She gave up and moved on to my other arm. Her previously failed attempts left my arm bruised for a month!

I had completely forgotten to call my doctor before we came in to the hospital! The nurse had to call a doctor who was on standby to come rushing in. My initial doctor had been very supportive of my birth plan at my prenatal appointments. Fortunately, the on-call doctor accepted my wishes. I wasn't nervous that another doctor would deliver my baby because she understood what I wanted. I felt that it was my job to tell her what my body was doing and when to push. I was in control of it! Since there were no complications, she let me guide the birth based on what my body was telling me to do.

By the time my husband finally returned with the camera, my body was ready to push even more! I remember looking at the clock, and it was 5:45 a.m. The first push was difficult because I didn't know exactly how hard I was supposed to push. Everyone was telling me I needed to try harder. The second and third pushes felt like nothing was happening. I refused the mirror when they asked if I would like to see what was going on down there. Unfortunately, my doctor had small glasses on; I couldn't help but glance at the reflection to see what it looked like. I saw a patch of dark hair with blood around it before quickly glancing the other way. My husband told me that the baby's head was halfway out and that the next push would be the end.

On that last push, I gave it my all! I screamed loudly, cursing like a sailor. And with that roar, out came my 5 lbs., 3 oz, 17.5 inch long baby girl at 6:06 a.m. Immediately, they put her on my chest for skin to skin contact, and I cried! What a beautiful moment it was!

Our blissful bonding lasted only ten minutes because I was told I was going to need stitches, and they wanted to get it done quickly. They provided local numbing anesthetic, but apparently it wasn't enough, because as they started stitching me up, I felt every little motion. I tell you, this was the worst I had to endure! Giving birth no longer seemed that painful compared to getting stitched up. I won't go into details, but let's just say everything felt excruciatingly raw. The good news was that even that part was over within ten minutes, and I was finally able to relax and have my fresh baby girl in my arms. My husband always knew I was capable of handling a lot, but it felt really amazing to have him witness the mental and physical strength I used to naturally birth our daughter.

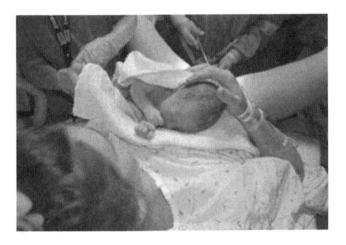

Looking back on my first birth experience, the labor was long, but once we arrived at the hospital, it felt like everything happened too fast! I wasn't able to really take in what was going on at the time. I actually *wanted* to do it all over again!

Baby Two

Five years later, my wish came true. I was pregnant and looking forward to another birthing experience. I had already done it once. I knew my mind and body could do it again, but that doesn't mean I wasn't nervous. Now I had a reference point from my first birth experience. Even though my first labor went pretty smoothly, I knew I wasn't guaranteed the same uncomplicated experience. Besides, I was told that the second baby comes faster than the first, and last time, we made it just before I started pushing. Thankfully, I still had that safety net that I lived just two minutes from the hospital.

BECAUSE YOU ARE SUPERWOMAN

Our second wish came true when my husband and I found out we were expecting a boy this time! I planned to let my body birth naturally like I did with my first born. I was full-term with my first baby, and she came out at 5 lbs., 3 oz. During all my checkups with the second baby, my doctor assured me that I would have another small baby…it turns out he was lucky his pay wasn't based on accuracy.

There were no real complications or problems during my second pregnancy. I did experience more heartburn and back aches than I did with my first born, but maybe that was a difference between a boy and a girl. On the positive side, I do remember feeling like I had more energy this time around.

During a check-up, the day before my due date, my doctor checked my cervix and told me I was 3 cm dilated. On that day, I experienced very little contractions and told myself I wasn't going to have this baby today. It was still March, and I wanted an April baby; I had actually planned it from the beginning. I also really wanted to avoid April Fool's Day on the first (which also happened to be the same day as Easter that year). Obviously, jokes and bets were made. Everyone predicted the first!

The day I was supposed to be due was definitely an off day. I barely had any contractions, and I was feeling amazing. I was excited to get my daughter's Easter stuff together that night and hide eggs for her. I wolfed down a good helping of Chinese food for dinner, and we put my daughter to bed early so I could get to work on her Easter goodies.

It was about 8:30 p.m. when I started laying everything out. I experienced a huge wave of hot flashes and then got extremely tired all of a sudden. I had this weird feeling that something wasn't right. I thought I had better try and get some rest. By this time, it was around 10:30 p.m. I was so tired, I thought for sure I was going to fall asleep quickly, but I was actually quite restless. It seemed a little crazy because there were no contractions, but I started telling myself this was it; it's happening!

The first of April, at 2:00 a.m., I woke up with a strong cramp and KNEW that this was it! I got up, went to the bathroom, and waited for another contraction, just in case I was dreaming it!

I was disappointed when nothing happened. I went back to bed and then it came again. It was even stronger, but not unbearable. I slapped my husband's knee and said, "It's happening!"

I got up in anticipation of the next contraction and started timing them myself. Ten minutes apart, forty-five seconds long. I waited until 3:00 a.m. to call my doctor. The nurse told me to come in when I was closer to 5–8 minutes apart.

Ten minutes after getting off the phone, the contractions had sped up and were rolling in every five minutes, forty-five seconds long. We took off right away. Fortunately, our hospital is only two minutes away from my house.

It was 3:40 a.m. when we walked in to the ER, signed in, and I was wheeled into the evaluation room. They dressed me into my gown, had me pee in a cup. and performed a cervix check. My contractions were still five minutes apart but growing stronger by the minute. The nurse told me that I was only 3–4 cm dilated! How could that be?!

They wheeled me into my delivery room and started prepping everything. For the next forty minutes, I laid in bed gripping the side railings during all the strong contractions I was having. At 4:30 a.m., they checked my cervix again, and this time, I was 8 cm dilated. Now we were finally getting somewhere!

Within a few minutes, I had a slight urge to push, and thought I felt my water break. My doctor finally came in and told me that my water had not broken yet, so she popped it.

My first push was super hard. My mouth was becoming so dry. I was constantly sucking on ice chips to breathe easier. I remember looking at the clock (4:40 a.m.) and wishing for the time to go by faster because the second push was even harder! I was feeling all the stretching and burning sensations down there. I knew I had to put my focus into something else, but the pain made it hard to do so.

The sensations of the third push were the worst yet. I ran out of breath while pushing. I tried to regain my breath, but instead I just screamed and cursed because I felt like I was tearing in half.

It is truly bizarre how you can go from that dark place to a moment of clarity once the contraction subsides. I had a moment to think while I waited for the next (and final!) contraction. I squeezed my eyes shut and focused on my breathing to distract myself from the intense sensations.

When that last push came, I absolutely gave it my all. My sweet boy slid out at 5:04 a.m. Immediately, he was put on my chest, and I held him for almost an hour.

They finally weighed him at 8 lbs., 7 oz. and 21 inches long. My first born was only 5 lbs., 3 oz. and 21 inches long, so there was a huge difference in the size of the two! We were absolutely shocked and amazed that my tiny frame pushed out such a big baby!

He was perfectly healthy and strong. We only stayed for one night at the hospital and went home the next day.

This labor felt incredibly short from start to finish. I feel grateful to end with this positive birth experience since I intend it to be my last. My mother taught me that my body was capable of giving birth with very minimal intervention. That's what I intend to teach my daughter. I hope that my stories help other women believe they are beyond capable!

BECAUSE YOU ARE SUPERWOMAN

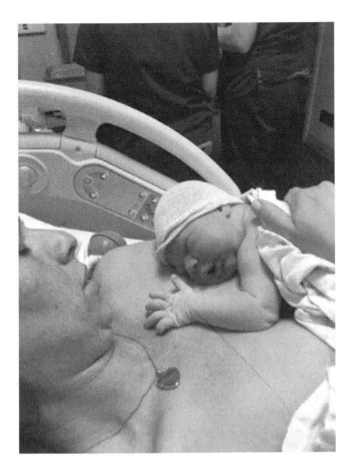

17 JACQUELYN'S BIRTH STORY: WHO SAYS A TWIN BIRTH MUST USE MAXIMUM INTERVENTIONS?

MEET JACQUELYN –

1. Education: bachelor's degree from University of Alaska (Anchorage), master's of business administration from Aspen University, National Midwifery Institute, International Board Certified Lactation Consultant (IBCLC)

2. Primary Job During Pregnancy: licensed midwife and IBCLC

3. Age at Delivery: 36

4. Two Ways I Prepared My Mind for Birth: Choosing to stay silent and confident

5. Two Ways I Prepared My Body for Birth: Yoga + walking

BECAUSE YOU ARE SUPERWOMAN

6. City/State of Birth: Venice, CA

7. Location of Birth: Home

8. Delivery Date: 40 weeks + 1 day

9. Present at Birth: One OB, one midwife, one student midwife, one filmmaker, husband

10. Did I Prefer Contractions or Pushing? Contractions. I never felt the urge to push.

11. Two Resources I Recommend to Others Preparing for Birth: Take prenatal yoga throughout pregnancy and learning about birth options and choices in childbirth.

12. Have I, or Would I, Aim for Another Minimal Intervention Birth After Experiencing It? Yes, I hope to birth again and this time, have a singleton!

13. My Empowering Message to Women Considering a Minimal Intervention Birth Plan: You can do it!

I was eight years old when my mother had my baby brother, attended by a midwife. He was a large baby at ten and a half pounds, but born naturally, without intervention. This early introduction to midwifery became a passion and led me to the profession.

When I first found out I was having twins, I was excited and knew I still wanted a home birth. I knew my pregnancy would be considered high risk, since I was over thirty-five and had two babies growing in my belly. I stayed fit, hydrated, well-nourished, and maintained a positive attitude, which I knew would keep my babies healthy and to term. I stress the importance of all of these to my clients who want to achieve their healthiest pregnancy. I walked at least two miles a day, did prenatal yoga 1–2 times a week, and I added in aquatic workouts the last month.

Originally from Alaska, I always thought about giving birth there, as place matters, and I wanted to share that lineage with my children. Yet as my healthy pregnancy progressed, it seemed less like a desirable option for me, butting heads with providers on the few visits I had there. I knew I would make it to full term; my babies were both head down, optimal positions for a natural birth, but I was still being told I may be offered a cesarean birth. So at thirty-five weeks, I made the decision to stay in Venice, CA for the opportunity to have the birth experience I desired.

In California, a home birth with twins is no longer legal with a licensed midwife. I considered using a hospital but finding someone who was experienced with twins and trusted in birth was really difficult. Unfortunately, I did not find a woman doctor, or any younger doctors (under sixty), who were comfortable with spontaneous labor (letting it occur naturally versus inducing at 37–38 weeks), and the opinions on breech twins varied as well. These professionals simply could not have the training that older doctors have had, which is unfortunate for the next generations to come.

Thankfully, I found an older, experienced doctor who offered a twin home birth option. As a certified professional midwife, I've worked with a couple twin families, as a student and while volunteering abroad. Because there weren't specialists available in these rural areas, those pregnancies were treated as a variation of "normal," simply siblings being born at the same time. Coupling that mindset with my midwifery training, I felt comfortable birthing my twins at home. Patient-centered, holistic care, informed consent, and education are core beliefs of midwifery. I am grateful to have learned these as part of my education.

Choosing a home birth is rare in this country, with only a small percentage of all births taking place out of hospital. Some friends and families were concerned whether I was making the right decision, but I weighed the risks and benefits, and home far outweighed the hospital. At a hospital, I would be strongly encouraged to have an epidural placed, "just in case," with delivery meant to be in the operating room. For many moms expecting multiples, a medical approach to their pregnancy also means mandatory induction from around 37 to 38 weeks for twins and even earlier with triplets or more. This did not sound appealing to me, nor conducive to having a natural birth! At home, I could wear my own clothes, would be free to eat and drink as needed, could move around—since monitoring is done intermittently

—and best of all, after the babies arrived, I would still be at home!

From thirty-six weeks until birth, standard prenatal schedule is weekly visits, unless more monitoring is required. I saw my home birth provider once a week, and my "backup" hospital doctor weekly as well. I did a non-stress test at thirty-eight weeks, where mom and babies are attached to a fetal monitor for a short time, and we all passed with flying colors!

On Saturday morning, just one day before my full-term due date, I woke up early with a mild cramp but was able to go back to sleep. Half an hour later, another one came.

A couple more sensations, and I knew labor had begun. I had a friend staying with us who was cooking in the kitchen, and my husband was doing clean-up from our recent home renovation. A fun aside, most couples I have worked with move or redo their home while pregnant! We had literally finished our bathroom the day before. I recall that we bickered about something—like where to store an item—and I nonchalantly said, I think the babies are coming today.

My water broke a few hours later, which brought contractions on more regularly. I made a thick horchata-like shake of brown rice, ice, and agave, and drank that throughout the day, snacking on frozen grapes. I listened to my babies and checked my vital signs periodically and everything stayed normal. Later that night, my provider came with a student midwife to check in. It was still early, which is such a frustrating thing to hear in labor! So they went home, and my house settled down for the night. Contractions continued regularly, but I was able to rest.

The next morning, the birth team checked in with us again. It was still early; in fact, contractions had slowed down, which is also common in first time labors. Early labor can stop and start, usually picking up more when night falls. At this point, we talked about different directions: ideas to pick it back up now or to try and rest before strongly encouraging labor later in the day. I opted for the second choice and set off to listen to a relaxing CD and then enjoy a bath.

Around 5:00 p.m., my midwife friend, who would be assisting my doctor, came by and was ready to get things moving. She had me drink some castor oil and juice, and we went for a walk around the neighborhood. It was Labor Day weekend, and we passed some holiday barbeques. One man exclaimed, "That woman is going to have a baby soon!"

"That's my goal!" I smiled.

Labor intensified over the next few hours, though everyone was getting tired. My husband started to question whether it was taking too long. I found out later he secretly packed a hospital bag. I told him I was fine, the babies sounded good, vital signs were normal, and we would be staying home. I agreed to another check, and I was complete.

From there, I never got the urge to push. Having been at hundreds of births, I knew a typical pattern to expect—active labor, transition, then pushing, and baby, but that wasn't my labor.

The team set up equipment and had me try pushing in a couple different positions: squatting, semi-reclining, laying down, but nothing really moved Baby A (who was already very low). The doctor told me he wanted to use a vacuum to assist with delivery because I didn't have an urge to push. Of course, I agreed; I trusted my OB and his expertise. A provider's skill is critical because using a vacuum at birth can be gentle or traumatic. The device manufacturer recommends a provider only attempts three passes with the vacuum attached. Mine worked immediately. With one long push, my son was born, and I pulled him up onto me.

With Baby A out, laying down felt so good. I basked in the

glow of being a parent of *just one* for the next twenty minutes. I checked to see that he was really a boy. The team reminded me to smile.

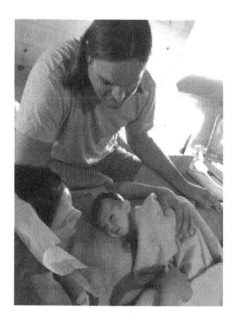

We listened to Baby B, and everything was perfect; three contractions later, my daughter was born. All in all, labor was forty-five hours start to finish.

The placentas fused together at some point late in pregnancy, and that was delivered without issue. My husband and I each cut an umbilical cord well after they had stopped pulsating. We opted for the Vitamin K injection since the vacuum had been used (which didn't seem to bother the babies at all). Vitamin K helps a baby's blood clot, since they are not born with the ability to do that naturally until around day eight. I also opted for a Pitocin injection, to help prevent bleeding, which is a possible complication with multiples. Then I requested an IV because I started to feel woozy. I required a few stitches, which was basically painless. Finally, I had an internal sweep for blood clots, which was uncomfortable and my least favorite part of labor and delivery!

The midwife and doctor did a newborn exam once we were settled in our clean bed, and everyone had been fed—babies included—and I had been kindly sponge-bathed. The babies were 6 lbs., 12 oz and 6 lbs., 13 oz, with a placenta weighing around 5 lbs.!

By then, our house had been cleared of birth matter, with the laundry started and everything put back in place. We were advised to put our phones on silent and enjoy a family nap. Someone would be back to check on us later that evening.

We were treated with love, and I truly believe everyone felt honored to be at this birth.

Birth is beautiful no matter how it occurs. It is transformative, more than any other life event, and even more so with the birth of two beings. Because I had professional experience with birth and knew what to expect, I wasn't afraid of natural birth, nor did I ever consider medication for pain.

I chose to be silent throughout labor, staying mostly in the privacy of my bathroom. It was peaceful and calm, and I drew strength from my family lineage.

I thought of my great grandmother who birthed nine children

in a rural Alaska cabin, without assistance or any modern comforts. I also thought of my mother who remembers my birth as fun because she knew what to expect (I was her second), and that birth is a unique life experience that we may only get to do a few times. I hope to have another birth experience, though next time with a singleton!

Motherhood is such an honor. I'm grateful to have had a positive birth experience and hope to inspire others by sharing my story.

18 JACLYN'S BIRTH STORIES: FROM FEARING BIRTH TO INSPIRING STORIES OF INTERVENTION-FREE BIRTHS

MEET JACLYN –

1. Education: bachelor's in Marketing and Management from Northwood University, master's in Elementary Education from University of Memphis

2. Primary Job During Pregnancy: Associate Director of Business Development for a CPG data marketing company

3. Age at Delivery: 33 and 35

4. Two Ways I Prepared My Mind for Birth: I read lots of positive birth stories in *Ina May's Guide to Childbirth*. I switched from an OB-GYN to a midwife. We discussed the mental aspects of giving birth, and I was encouraged to discuss anything I was nervous about.

5. Two Ways I Prepared My Body for Birth: I kept active

through both pregnancies, running until the third trimester, then walking or hiking. I also did light weights, squats, and body weight movements until the day I gave birth. Toward the end of pregnancy, I enjoyed massages to relax and align my body before delivery.

6. City/State of Birth: Laguna Hills, CA (both)

7. Location of Birth: Saddleback Memorial Hospital (both)

8. Delivery Date: Baby One: 40 weeks + 6 days, Baby Two: 41 weeks + 3 days

9. Present at Birth: Baby One: midwife, two nurses, a group of medical students who wanted to observe an unmedicated birth, and my husband. Baby Two: midwife, three nurses who rushed in, and my husband.

10. Did I Prefer Contractions or Pushing? Baby One: Contractions, Baby Two: Pushing

11. Two Resources I Recommend to Others Preparing for Birth: Read *Ina May's Guide to Childbirth*. Actively seek out a midwife or OB-GYN who regularly practices delivering babies with minimal intervention, advocating only for interventions that are necessary and proven to be in the best interest of the mother and baby.

12. Have I, or Would I, Aim for Another Minimal Intervention Birth After Experiencing It? I have done it twice and would do it again. It's not easy, but I didn't regret my choices before, during, or after delivery. Overall, it has made

me more confident in my ability to handle difficult situations.

13. My Empowering Message to Women Considering a Minimal Intervention Birth Plan: I fully believe you are capable of giving birth to your baby. Do not let fear guide you. Seek out stories and advice from those who have achieved what you want. Do not try to rush things. Believe that your baby and body will coordinate the perfect time. Educate yourself, then hang on and enjoy the ride!

Birth One

Not everyone wants a natural childbirth. DUH, I get it.

But I'm confident that every mother wants a positive birth experience. The funny thing is, most of us aren't exposed to many, if ANY, positive birth stories before we have to give birth ourselves.

We assume they don't exist because of how the media portrays birth, or because people are so damn eager to share their horror stories, or because it's just not the norm. So, I wanted to share my birth stories, as a point of positive reference.

Does that mean I am going to tell you that birth is glamorous, something I'd chose to do for fun, or pain free? I wish. Really, I do. It would make it easier for us both, especially since I plan to have more babies. But I have learned the strength that giving birth can provide a woman. And that can be a very positive, empowering experience. It can shape how she views life from that day forward.

So here we go: the birth story of a mother, a father, and a baby. Because that is the thing, you birth a baby and a new identity for yourself and your significant other, all at the same time. It's crazy to think about, *right*?!

At thirty-three years old, I finally felt like I had traveled, learned, and self-indulged long enough that I was ready for a child. Fortunately, my husband was also far beyond his college party days, willingly going to bed by 10:00 p.m., and on board with the baby idea.

After four months of finally trying to conceive, I took three pregnancy tests the day before Father's Day and confirmed I was, in fact, with child. Why three tests? I messed up the first one by not reading the directions (Yup, it can be more complicated than peeing on a stick—you have to remove the cover), the second was a false negative, and the third was a winner! I got to surprise my husband, on his first official Father's Day, with a "Rad Like Dad" onesie.

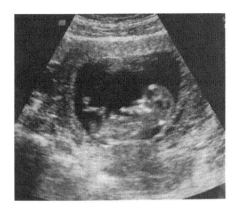

Once we found out we were pregnant, I started down the traditional health care path. I picked an OB-GYN, and as it turned out, I really liked her. She was younger, active, and had two young kids. I had no issues.

During the first trimester, I was tired and found myself taking naps for the first time in years. By the second trimester, things were back to normal. Throughout pregnancy, I took my prenatal vitamins, tried to get daily exercise, consumed "real food" along with my normal intake of dark chocolate treats, and often spent evening hours soaking in our bathtub. I felt good during the third trimester and continued to stay as active as possible. I gave up running around thirty-two weeks because it was taking my body an extra day to recover after a few miles, but I was still playing tennis, walking, doing light weights, and a little Zumba.

My belly was growing pretty big, and it was time I got serious about learning what my body was about to experience, whether I was ready or not. The more I learned about birth in the U.S. (routine interventions like: epidurals, Pitocin, cesareans, birthing on our back, being bound to the bed, catheters, not eating...), the more I started to think about natural birth and the idea of trusting in my body and birthing with as few interventions as possible. Honestly, I wasn't 100% convinced I was capable of going that route, but once I found out that there was a midwife who took a more holistic approach to birth *and* could deliver at my hospital, I switched to her care at thirty-three weeks. I figured it was my best chance of receiving the coaching and attention I felt I would need to achieve the minimal intervention birth I wanted.

I worked up until my due date. Since baby hadn't arrived yet, I decided to start my maternity leave and focus on my to-do list. I went in for an appointment at 40 weeks + 3 days. I

BECAUSE YOU ARE SUPERWOMAN

wasn't dilated a bit. But, I figured my baby and body knew what to do when, so I wasn't too worried until the midwife started discussing inserting a balloon to start dilation. I was not excited. She said she would give me a few more days.

At 40 weeks + 5 days, I went to Zumba. I enjoyed rocking out with my baby, and I am sure everyone else enjoyed watching the crazy pregnant woman shake it. Not that I cared at that point!

I had finished everything on my to-do list, so I decided to lay out by the pool. That was noon on Leap Day, the one day my husband told me not to have the baby. I felt what I thought may be the start of contractions, but I decided to relax and see.

By 6:00 p.m., when my husband came home from work, I told him I thought I was in labor. Since contractions were still far enough apart, I decided to go to sleep around 9:00 p.m. After an hour, they were getting stronger and closer, and I started tracking them with an iPhone app called "Full Term." I got up, took a bath, packed my bag, paced the house, sat on the exercise ball, and used a heating pad on my back. By 5:00 a.m., we texted the midwife to let her know I was in labor. We left the house about 6:15 a.m., arriving at the hospital by 6:30 a.m. When I walked in, they said I seemed too calm to be in labor. On the inside, I didn't feel calm! I was in pain and just trying to deal with it internally. I was offered a wheelchair but declined. Mentally, it felt better to keep moving.

When they checked me at 7:15 a.m., they asked if I wanted an epidural. I said, "That depends, how far along am I?" I was at 5 cm. I decided to press on.

Once I got into my hospital room, I was able to pace around the room and lean on various furniture or my husband for support when the contractions hit. Once the midwife arrived, she applied counter pressure on my back during each contraction. She told me I could try out the labor tub at 8:45 a.m. At this hospital, you could labor in it until your water broke, then you had to get out because of increased risk of infection.

By that point, contractions were very intense. I was groaning, as I could feel the baby moving down with every contraction and the pressure and intensity building. Honestly, I don't know if I was totally coherent at that point. I was just trying to block everything out. Thankfully, my husband recorded all the times and details in a notebook once we reached the hospital. Without that, there is no way I could accurately string the timing of events together.

I do remember that I was no longer a sweet pregnant woman by the time my midwife told me that I needed to get out of the tub so that she could check me (9:50 a.m.). I was more of a barbaric, naked, grunting beast. She said the sounds of my groans had changed, and it was a signal that my body was likely ready to push. I needed to abandon the tub, my Zen place to moan alone. I wanted to put my hands around her neck and squeeze, except that would have taken too much energy and coordination, which I didn't have at that moment.

Somehow, I exited the tub, and they checked me. Apparently, that was when my water broke. I was 10 cm (10:20 a.m.). I was ready to push.

I had imagined that I would want to push standing up, with the help of gravity working with me. But once I was on the bed to get checked, there was no way I was moving. Instead, I chose a side position, biting a towel, with one of my legs propped up on a push bar for leverage. By that point, my contractions were off the charts; I was screaming at their peak and squeezing my husband's hand like a stress ball. My body was starting to push involuntarily. I was nervous and began using my energy to fight back against the urge.

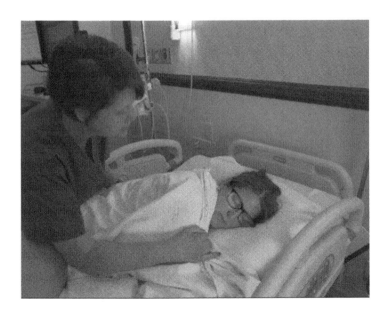

Eventually, I was told that the high-pitched screams weren't helping anything. Plus, I started to worry that I was scaring the laboring mother in the next room. My midwife suggested that I use low groans, then hold my breath and use the power to push my baby out.

They told me they could see the baby's head. I figured they were just trying to humor me at that point. They asked if I wanted a mirror so that I could see for myself. I declined. I don't like medical situations and there was no way I wanted to see what was going on down there while I was in the middle of it and had no option to stop the moving train. Some people say the pushing phase feels good after the pain of contractions. That was not my experience. The amount of pressure down there felt scary. To be a bit graphic, I felt like I was tearing in half. I tried to crawl into my body to avoid really pushing.

But here is the crazy thing. Through all of this, asking for an epidural never crossed my mind. With the constant attention and affirming coaching from my husband and midwife, I felt convinced that this was all normal. This was how birth was supposed to progress. I could just get through it one moment at a time. My body was not broken. I did not need a doctor to fix me. What I needed was a calm environment, love and support, gentle coaching to try new things (positions, breathing, etc.), and a belief in myself. But had someone been in my ear asking if I wanted an epidural or left me alone with my fears, I probably would have cracked.

Finally, I re-centered and got serious about pushing. I was stuck at that point, and there was only one way out. I had to go toward the pain to get it over with. After pushing for three quarters of an hour, the head started to emerge. I was ready for all this fun to be over. During the next contraction, I pushed with all my might, and the rest of the head and body slid out at 11:08 a.m. My midwife and husband were there to catch the baby.

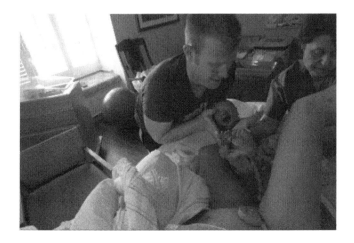

She was perfect. I couldn't believe it. The pain was over. The pain had a purpose. The pain told my body what to do. And that purpose was now in my arms.

I had some tearing, so I had to wait until I delivered the placenta and got stitched up before I finally got to be left alone between my legs. But once I was, it was awesome. I wasn't attached to anything. I could freely move and bond with my daughter, soaking up those first few hours as a new little family.

I was pretty damn proud of the birth my daughter and I just achieved by trusting each other and working together.

Our first amazing adventure, on day one.

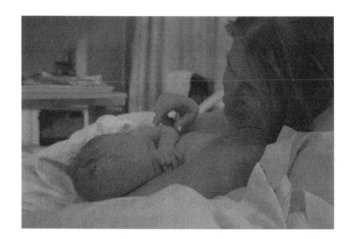

Birth Two

My second birth story opened in a seedy nail salon in a strip-mall in Orange County, CA. It was the type of nail place you go when you've already spent too much money on personal grooming that month, and you need a deal. Adequate but so dated that it's far from a relaxing and luxurious experience. There was a woman painting my toes and massaging my feet, as I quietly tried to breathe through contractions without causing a scene.

At that point, I was ten days "past due," which in my opinion, is not as big of a deal as people like to make it. Especially since I knew my baby's due date was a weaker guesstimate than normal because my period hadn't returned yet. When I conceived, I was still enjoying breastfeeding my thirteen-month-old to bed (which is exciting to report since my daughter getting anywhere near my boobs brought me to tears in the early months). But you never know what is going on under the hood.

I found out I was pregnant…in a bathroom stall at work… during my last two weeks there. I had resigned a week prior. Yes, it is *almost* humorous now, but on that particular day, not so much. We had always wanted more children, but two in less than two years wasn't exactly calculated.

Timing aside, I felt blessed on a daily basis that everything was progressing well. I was more tired the second time around, but I did have a toddler! I maintained another active pregnancy (running, walking, tennis, weights), but I was feeling pretty big after gaining ten more pounds than I had with my last pregnancy.

I planned to deliver with the same midwife in the same hospital. Things went well the first time around, so I felt no need to change it. I did, however, make sure to reread all the positive natural birth stories, because this time I knew what birth was like, and I needed to have my head on straight when the day came.

Since I had gone past my due date, and I was of advanced maternal age at approximately thirty-five years and three months, I was going to two appointments a week to check the fluid levels around the baby and her activity. We continued to pass with flying colors, so they let my body continue to care for my little girl. However, the majority of birth professionals and locations come with their own expiration date, and eventually, they try to kick you into gear. As I surpassed 40 weeks + 6 days, they made me schedule an induction for the evening of 41 weeks + 6 days (the latest possible date my midwife would agree to).

At 41 weeks + 2 days, I was still on the fence whether I would show up to my induction or not. They were regularly confirming that my baby and I were doing well, I believed my little girl knew when to arrive, and I really felt my due date was a best guess, not an expiration date.

I went to bed with some minor back pain. In the morning, it

BECAUSE YOU ARE SUPERWOMAN

was still mild, so I spent a few hours working on one of my children's books and making no-bake coconut bites. Then I took a two-mile walk, washed and vacuumed my car, and bought a new house plant, before finally heading to the nail salon at 2:30 p.m. By then, I had convinced myself that I was likely in labor, but I figured I had plenty of time since the pain was manageable and hadn't come around to the front of my belly yet. It was all still in my back.

So, back at the nail salon, another woman started doing my gel manicure. I'm pretty sure it must have been her first gel because it took her over an hour. She kept applying the paint, then wiping it off and starting over.

Mind you, this entire time, the back contractions were continuing to intensify. I was shooting the woman daggers with my eyes, praying she would get it together so I could go home and be miserable in peace. I finally asked her if she was almost done because I had to go; this baby was coming tonight. Every ten minutes, I was having a thirty second contraction that I had to close my eyes to breathe through.

By 4:00 p.m. she finally wrapped it up. I drove myself home and was in the tub by 4:15 p.m. My husband came into the bathroom to check on me. I told him what was going on but figured the contractions needed to get closer together before heading to the hospital. I was planning another natural birth, with as little intervention as possible, so the last thing I wanted to do was arrive at the hospital too early.

251

I reached out to my midwife just to let her know that I thought we would be heading in to the hospital later that night. I decided to track the contractions with the Full Term app on my phone. Come to find out, I am a poor counter while in pain. The contractions that I thought were thirty seconds long were really a minute, every eight to ten minutes apart.

I showered between contractions while my husband made arrangements for our toddler. Then I decided to go lay in bed. My poor husband tried to push on my back during a contraction because the counter-pressure during contractions had been really helpful with my first labor. This time, not so much. Laying down and having someone push on my back was the exact opposite of comforting. Contractions were lasting about a minute and a half, every four to six minutes, at that point. He asked where it was best for him to push; I was almost in tears and snapped at him to stop asking me so many questions!

That was my first cue that we probably needed to head to the hospital. That, and the fact that the intensity of the contractions was getting to the point where I could no longer quietly breathe through them. I was moaning out in pain. We headed out to the car for our four-mile drive to the hospital.

During the ten-minute drive, I was alternating between texting my parents who had just arrived at LAX airport (an hour away), giving updates to my midwife—contractions were now lasting for one minute—every three minutes, listtening to my husband yell at every stop light, and squeezing my cell phone like a stress ball as I moaned through contractions. I'm sure my husband was grateful that it was my phone, and not his hand this time. As we rounded the corner by the hospital, a very intense contraction got me, and I firmly pounded my fist on the car door a few times. That got my husband's attention. This labor had gotten REAL really fast.

Once at the hospital, I jumped out of the car while my husband grabbed our bags. I had to pause at a couch inside the lobby to moan through another contraction. There was a man and his young son nearby, and I was trying my best not to be too loud and scare them. By then, my husband caught up with me and was trying to get me to take the elevator up to the birthing level.

"Nope," I said. I needed to keep moving. I had one goal. Make it to the nurse's station before the next contraction.

"I'm taking the stairs."

Thankfully, I did, because I literally made it to the nurse's station, saw my midwife behind the counter and smiled at her, then put my head down telling the triage nurse to talk to my husband for any details she needed. I started moaning through another contraction, except this time, it was different. I could feel my body start to involuntarily push the baby down. It was like my body knew I had made it. I was in the hospital. My midwife was there. I was safe. The time was 6:08 p.m.

As soon as my midwife heard the types of sounds I was making, she took over the situation. She told the nurses to get me a room NOW. They offered me a chair to wheel me to a room.

"Nope," I said. I wanted to walk since I had a break between contractions.

We made it to a room. They had me take off my pants and offered me a hospital gown.

"Nope," I said. I didn't want to feel like a patient.

The nurses told me I could climb up on the bed.

"Nope."

I was a woman on a mission at that point; my one and only job was to birth this baby, NOW.

"Hand me those pillows," I said to the nurse.

That was the last rational thing I said until my baby arrived. I proceeded to stand next to the bed, lean over, and bury my face in the pillows while I screamed through each contraction as my body pushed the baby down and out. I knew I was supposed to be trying to keep my voice low and relaxed, but all I could do was shrill and hang on for the ride.

Somehow, my husband was able to get the video camera set up during all this (in case you're wondering, it's not a flattering angle). He then asked the midwife how much time we had before the baby arrived. She confidently whispered, "About two more pushes."

She was right. Two pushes later, she and my husband were catching a perfect baby girl. I laid over the bed panting as if I had just finished a marathon in record time. They offered to pass the baby through my legs so I could hold her and get up on the bed. Official time of birth—6:16 p.m.

Yup, *eight minutes* after arriving at the nurse's station.

I'm not sure if that was a hospital record, but my IRONMAN husband is looking in to it. He laughs, because on the video, he says it's like I have a race high. I am really excited and can't stop jabbering with the nurses about what just happened. In my defense there were a lot of endorphins and hormones rushing through my body at that point.

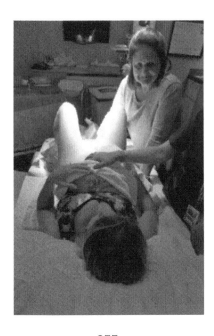

An hour and a half later, the medical staff was finally done prodding my lower half, checking on the baby, and making me answer hospital in-take questions—since we bypassed that last bit on the way in. As they walked out, my parents arrived from LAX.

After a short visit with my parents, we sent them out to get Pizza Hut, the holy grail of postpartum. The restaurant was located just a mile away, and they were supposed to deliver the pizza to my parents, downstairs at the main entrance of the hospital. Somehow, it took over an hour, and they ended up delivering the wrong pizza! I thought about calling to complain, but it was 10:00 p.m., and I hadn't eaten since 1:00 p.m., so obviously I just grumbled about it as I ate three pieces. The good news was that it bought us a proper moment to meet our baby girl and finally agree on a name.

Baby Liv Claire Coy entered our world fast and furious. A crazy yet perfect labor and delivery. Definitely the most exciting Friday night these parents have had in a long time.

BECAUSE YOU ARE SUPERWOMAN

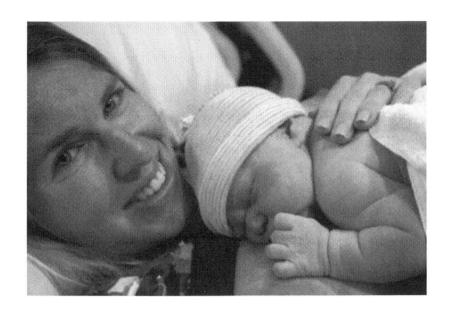

19 GET EXCITED, BECAUSE YOU WERE MADE FOR THIS!

As a woman, you get approximately forty weeks to anticipate the experience of giving birth. During my most recent pregnancy, I actually got forty weeks and ten days, but who's counting?

The journey to meeting your sweet baby can feel very long. You deserve to feel happy with your experience during both pregnancy and labor. How you feel about birth matters. The birth choices you make matter. How you are treated by your care providers matters. Your birth story matters.

Keep filling your head with positive and realistic examples of birth, and share them if you have them. Get used to asking questions when a suggested intervention doesn't quite make sense. Make sure your practitioner is comfortable and experienced in supporting, not controlling, a woman's body. And don't be afraid to go about birth your own way. You don't have to do it the way your mom, or your sister-in-law, or your best friend did it.

Every woman in this book has been right where you are now, sometimes struggling to believe in herself as labor draws near. Please know they didn't possess any superpower that you don't already have, that allowed them to magically have the positive, minimal intervention birth experience that they wanted. They simply understood that their birth beliefs and choices would have a profound impact on their birth story. And they took charge.

You are now equipped with the six steps to a Minimal Intervention (M.I.) Birth, so you have a game plan. Having a plan will give you the confidence to shut down that little voice in your head that pops up and tries to convince you that you are not strong enough and not capable enough, to achieve a more natural, minimal intervention birth. There is no reason for you to believe that you can't have a positive and empowering experience.

One more thing, since we are friends now and we can let our guard down, it's okay to feel anxious about the idea of a watermelon exiting a donut. Don't worry. It's science and a miracle wrapped in one. We don't have to fully understand how, just know that it happens safely every day!

Your body was literally created to do this.

Go look in the mirror and smile.

Damn girl, you've got superwoman inside you.

I WANT TO HEAR FROM YOU!

I am Woman, hear me ROAR!

<u>Please consider leaving a quick and honest review on Amazon right now.</u>

Your voice has the potential to help women find this book and empower their birth!

Spread the love online:
#BecauseYouAreSuperwoman, #MIBirth, @StoriesbyJKCoy

READ MORE TITLES BY J.K. COY

Love You to Pieces, Beautiful Monster

From the moment this beautiful monster wakes, the rollercoaster ride begins. *Love You to Pieces, Beautiful Monster* describes the emotional roller coaster ride that is lovingly referred to as: A Day in the Life of Parenting Young Children. "Every day you make me crazy, I love you to pieces, Beautiful Monster."

My Mom is the Worst

Are you the worst parent?! Do you make your child wear underwear? Or take a bath?! You probably even hug them so tightly they can't get away sometimes! Your child is sure to find this tale of what parents DO TO THEIR KIDS extremely funny, as they will surely relate to the everyday situations.

ABOUT THE AUTHOR

J.K. Coy became a mother to two daughters in less than two years, so obviously, she doesn't sit still well. She originally hails from Michigan, but after moving to Southern California over seven years ago, she now considers California her second home.

Her adorable and humorous children's books are enjoyed by both parents and their little ones: *Love You to Pieces Beautiful Monster* (2016) and *My Mom is the Worst* (2017). She is also the creator of the Minimal Intervention (M.I.) Birth Method designed to provide evidence-based steps and inspiring stories to help women achieve more positive birth experiences using minimal medical intervention.

She holds a bachelor's in business and a master's in elementary education. During the brief moments between her roles as a corporate climber, mom, and wife, she enjoys sharpening her creative pencil.

Her intent is to entertain the parent and child at the same time. Sometimes it's the little joys and inside jokes that get everyone through another bedtime routine.

RESOURCES

American College of Obstetricians and Gynecologists (ACOG), Approaches to Limit Intervention During Labor and Birth:
https://www.acog.org/Clinical-Guidance-and-Publications/Committee-Opinions/Committee-on-Obstetric-Practice/Approaches-to-Limit-Intervention-During-Labor-and-Birth

Center for Disease Control (CDC), Birth Data:
https://www.cdc.gov/nchs/nvss/births.htm

Center for Disease Control (CDC), Meeting the Challenges of Measuring and Preventing Maternal Mortality in the United States:
https://www.cdc.gov/grand-rounds/pp/2017/20171114-maternal-mortality.html

Doulamatch.net

Epstein, Abby. 2008. Movie: *The Business of Being Born.*

May, Ina. 2003. *Ina May's Guide to Childbirth (Paperback).* New York: Bantam.

Midwife Alliance of North America: https://mana.org/

National Partnership for Women and Families, Listening to Mothers Reports and Surveys: http://www.nationalpartnership.org/research-library/maternal-health/listening-to-mothers-iii-pregnancy-and-birth-2013.pdf

National Partnership for Women and Families, The Cost of Having a Baby in the United States: http://www.nationalpartnership.org/research-library/maternal-health/the-cost-of-having-a-baby-in-the-us.pdf

Oster, Emily. 2014. *Expecting Better: Why the Conventional Pregnancy Wisdom Is Wrong--and What You Really Need to Know.* New York: Penguin Books.

World Health Organization (WHO), Statement on Cesarean Section Rates: http://www.who.int/reproductivehealth/publications/maternal_perinatal_health/cs-statement/en/

Please visit MyMomistheWorst.com

for more stories and products related to or mentioned in this book.

Made in the USA
Middletown, DE
21 February 2019